Cisco Networking Academy Program

Fundamentals of Wireless LANs
Engineering Journal and Workbook

Cisco Systems, Inc.

Cisco Networking Academy Program

Cisco Press

800 East 96th Street, 3rd Floor
Indianapolis, Indiana 46240 USA

Cisco Networking Academy Program
Fundamentals of Wireless LANs Engineering Journal and Workbook

Cisco Systems, Inc.
Cisco Networking Academy Program

Copyright © 2004 Cisco Systems, Inc.

Published by:
Cisco Press
201 West 103rd Street
Indianapolis, IN 46290 USA

Printed in the United States of America   1 2 3 4 5 6 7 8 9 0
First Printing   September 2003

ISBN: 1-58713-120-X

Warning and Disclaimer

This book is designed to provide information on wireless LAN fundamentals. Every effort has been made to make this book as complete and as accurate as possible, but no warranty or fitness is implied.

The information is provided on an as-is basis. The author, Cisco Press, and Cisco Systems, Inc., shall have neither liability nor responsibility to any person or entity with respect to any loss or damages arising from the information contained in this book or from the use of the discs or programs that may accompany it.

The opinions expressed in this book belong to the author and are not necessarily those of Cisco Systems, Inc.

This book is part of the Cisco Networking Academy® Program series from Cisco Press. The products in this series support and complement the Cisco Networking Academy Program curriculum. If you are using this book outside the Networking Academy program, then you are not preparing with a Cisco trained and authorized Networking Academy provider.

For information on the Cisco Networking Academy Program or to locate a Networking Academy, please visit www.cisco.com/edu.

Trademark Acknowledgments

All terms mentioned in this book that are known to be trademarks or service marks have been appropriately capitalized. Cisco Press or Cisco Systems, Inc., cannot attest to the accuracy of this information. Use of a term in this book should not be regarded as affecting the validity of any trademark or service mark.

Feedback Information

At Cisco Press, our goal is to create in-depth technical books of the highest quality and value. Each book is crafted with care and precision, undergoing rigorous development that involves the unique expertise of members from the professional technical community.

Readers' feedback is a natural continuation of this process. If you have any comments regarding how we could improve the quality of this book, or otherwise alter it to better suit your needs, you can contact us at networkingacademy@ ciscopress.com. Please make sure to include the book title and ISBN in your message.

We greatly appreciate your assistance.

Publisher	John Wait
Editor-in-Chief	John Kane
Cisco Systems Representative	Anthony Wolfenden
Cisco Press Program Manager	Sonia Torres Chavez
Cisco Marketing Communications Manager	Scott Miller
Cisco Marketing Program Manager	Edie Quiroz
Production Manager	Patrick Kanouse
Acquisitions Editor	Sarah Kimberly
Senior Development Editor	Christopher Cleveland
Senior Project Editor	Sheri Cain
Copy Editor	Karen A. Gill

CISCO SYSTEMS

Corporate Headquarters	European Headquarters	Americas Headquarters	Asia Pacific Headquarters
Cisco Systems, Inc.	Cisco Systems International BV	Cisco Systems, Inc.	Cisco Systems, Inc.
170 West Tasman Drive	Haarlerbergpark	170 West Tasman Drive	Capital Tower
San Jose, CA 95134-1706	Haarlerbergweg 13-19	San Jose, CA 95134-1706	168 Robinson Road
USA	1101 CH Amsterdam	USA	#22-01 to #29-01
www.cisco.com	The Netherlands	www.cisco.com	Singapore 068912
Tel: 408 526-4000	www-europe.cisco.com	Tel: 408 526-7660	www.cisco.com
800 553-NETS (6387)	Tel: 31 0 20 357 1000	Fax: 408 527-0883	Tel: +65 6317 7777
Fax: 408 526-4100	Fax: 31 0 20 357 1100		Fax: +65 6317 7799

Cisco Systems has more than 200 offices in the following countries and regions. Addresses, phone numbers, and fax numbers are listed on the
Cisco.com Web site at www.cisco.com/go/offices.

Argentina • Australia • Austria • Belgium • Brazil • Bulgaria • Canada • Chile • China PRC • Colombia • Costa Rica • Croatia • Czech Republic Denmark • Dubai, UAE • Finland • France • Germany • Greece • Hong Kong SAR • Hungary • India • Indonesia • Ireland • Israel • Italy Japan • Korea • Luxembourg • Malaysia • Mexico • The Netherlands • New Zealand • Norway • Peru • Philippines • Poland • Portugal Puerto Rico • Romania • Russia • Saudi Arabia • Scotland • Singapore • Slovakia • Slovenia • South Africa • Spain • Sweden Switzerland • Taiwan • Thailand • Turkey • Ukraine • United Kingdom • United States • Venezuela • Vietnam • Zimbabwe

Table of Contents

Preface

Since 1997, the Cisco Networking Academy Program has instituted an e-learning model that integrates the multimedia delivery of a networking curriculum with testing, performance-based skills assessment, evaluation, and reporting through a web interface. The Networking Academy curriculum goes beyond traditional computer-based instruction by helping students develop practical networking knowledge and skills in a hands-on environment. In a lab setting that closely corresponds to a real networking environment, students work with the architecture and infrastructure pieces of networking technology. As a result, students learn the principles and practices of networking technology.

The Cisco Networking Academy Program provides in-depth and meaningful networking content, which is being used by regional and local academies to teach students around the world by using the curriculum to integrate networking instruction into the classroom. The focus of the Networking Academy is on the integration of a web-based network curriculum into the learning environment. This element is addressed through intensive staff development for instructors and innovative classroom materials and approaches to instruction, which Cisco provides. Cisco Systems provides participating educators with resources, the means of remote access to online support, and the knowledge base for the effective classroom integration of the Networking Academy curriculum into the classroom learning environment. As a result, the Cisco Networking Academy Program provides the means for the dynamic exchange of information by providing a suite of services that redefine the way instructional resources are disseminated, resulting in a many-to-many interactive and collaborative network of teachers and students functioning to meet diverse educational needs.

The Networking Academy curriculum is especially exciting to educators and students because the courseware is interactive. Because of the growing use of interactive technologies, the curriculum is a new way to convey instruction with new interactive technologies that allow instructors and trainers to mix a number of media, including audio, video, text, numerical data, and graphics. Consequently, students can select different media from the computer screen and tweak their instructional content to meet their instructional needs, and educators have the option of either designing their own environment for assessment or selecting from the applicable assessments.

Finally, by developing a curriculum that recognizes the changing classroom and workforce demographics, the globalization of the economy, changing workforce knowledge and skill requirements, and the role of technology in education, the Cisco Networking Academy Program supports national educational goals for K–12 education. As support for the Cisco Networking Academy Program, Cisco Press published this book, *Cisco Networking Academy Program Fundamentals of Wireless LANs Engineering Journal and Workbook*, to further complement the curriculum used in the Cisco Networking Academy Program.

Introduction

Cisco Networking Academy Program Fundamentals of Wireless LANs Engineering Journal and Workbook supplements your classroom and laboratory experience with the Cisco Networking Academy Program, whose curriculum empowers you to enter employment or further education and training in the computer networking field.

This tool further trains you beyond the online course materials that you have already used in this program, and helps prepare you for the Cisco Wireless LAN Support Specialist (WLANFE). This book closely follows the style and format that Cisco Systems has incorporated into the curriculum. *Cisco Networking Academy Program Fundamentals of Wireless LANs Engineering Journal and Workbook* provides you with additional exercises and activities that reinforce your learning. Also included are writing opportunities that help you learn to establish and keep an engineering journal.

It is recommend that you keep a technical or engineering journal. Typically, a journal is a paper-bound composition book in which pages are not added or subtracted, but dated. The types of journal entries most applicable for Networking Academy students include daily reflections, troubleshooting details, lab procedures and observations, equipment logs, hardware and software notes, and router configurations. Because the journal becomes more important as you do more network design and installation work, good habits can be developed by starting with a journal on the first day of the Fundamentals of Wireless LANs course. In this book, you are asked to keep your journal on a daily basis.

Chapter 1

Introduction to Wireless LANs

This chapter introduces you to the rapidly evolving wireless technologies. Wireless signals are electromagnetic waves, which can travel as well in the vacuum of space as they do through the air in an office building. The ability of radio waves to pass through walls and cover great distances makes wireless technology a versatile way to build a network.

The following are advantages to wireless local-area networks (WLANs):
- Mobility
- Scalability
- Flexibility
- Short- and long-term cost savings
- Installation advantages
- Reliability in harsh environments
- Reduced installation time

Although WLANs are primarily designed as LAN devices, they can be used to provide site-to-site connectivity at distances up to 25 miles. WLAN devices are much more cost effective than using WAN bandwidth or installing or leasing long fiber runs.

The medium of wireless fits on the bottom rung of the OSI protocol model, along with wires and fibers of all types. This chapter quickly reviews the different types of networking media that are used at the physical layer, including shielded twisted-pair (STP) cable, unshielded twisted-pair (UTP) cable, coaxial cable, fiber-optic cable, and propagated radio waves, which is the medium used by wireless technologies.

Wireless uses a sophisticated modulation system called *spread spectrum*. Spread spectrum spreads a transmission signal over a broad range of radio frequencies. This technique is ideal for data communications because it is less susceptible to radio noise and creates little interference. Spread spectrum comes in two forms:
- Frequency hopping spread spectrum (FHSS)
- Direct sequence spread spectrum (DSSS)

When you are designing and building networks, always make certain that you comply with all applicable fire codes, building codes, and safety standards. Follow any established performance standards to ensure optimal network operation. Be sure to consider compatibility and interoperability, including choice of wireless equipment. Older systems use 802.11b, and newer systems use 802.11a and 802.11g. This chapter discusses the differences, uses, and advantages of each.

There is still a lot that is not known concerning the safe limits of human exposure to radio frequency (RF) radiation. The best and easiest general rule is not to subject living things unnecessarily to radiated RF energy. This means that you should avoid standing in front of or in close proximity to any antenna that is radiating a transmitted signal. Safety precautions with radio energy are discussed in this chapter.

Innovative wireless solutions help solve market-specific problems:

- **Manufacturing**—Wireless technology is used to access manufacturer recommended price and inventory management systems from the shop floor.
- **Healthcare**—Wireless technology gives doctors and nurses access to real-time patient care information at the bedside.
- **Retail**—Wireless technology enables salespeople to make inventory checks without leaving the storefront.
- **Education**—Wireless technology enables students and teachers to be connected to learning resources in campus environments composed of historical structures.

Concept Questions

1. What is spread spectrum modulation and what are its advantages?

   _____

   _____

   _____

   _____

2. How is optical fiber different from wired media?

   _____

   _____

   _____

   _____

3. What is the difference between UTP and various forms of STP?

   _____

   _____

   _____

   _____

   _____

4. What must you do when routing a cable to a wireless access point if the intended route passed through a wall designated to be a firewall?

   _____

   _____

_____
_____
_____

5.   What are some definitions of "radio"?

_____
_____
_____
_____
_____

6.   Describe an ad hoc topology.

_____
_____
_____
_____
_____

7.   Describe the three power consumption modes that are available with Cisco
       PC cards, and the situations where each would be used.

_____
_____
_____
_____
_____

8.   What are some of the environments that are likely to benefit from
       implementation of WLAN?

_____
_____
_____
_____
_____

9.   What are some of the characteristics of electromagnetic waves?

_____
_____
_____
_____
_____

10.   What are some of the advantages of using a wireless connection between
       two buildings?

_____
_____
_____

11   List and describe the factors that influence the growing acceptance of wireless technology.

_____

_____

_____

_____

_____

12   What are some safety precautions that need to be taken when working around RF radiation?

_____

_____

_____

_____

_____

Vocabulary Exercise

128-bit encryption

_____

_____

_____

_____

802.11

_____

_____

_____

802.11b

_____

_____

_____

access point

_____

_____

_____

ad hoc network

_____
_____
_____
_____

AM

_____
_____
_____
_____

AMPS

_____
_____
_____
_____

antenna

_____
_____
_____
_____

antenna selection

_____
_____
_____
_____

authorized spectrum

_____
_____
_____
_____

background noise

_____
_____
_____
_____

backwards compatibility

_____
_____

bandwidth

Bluetooth

bps

broadband

bridge

CAM

carrier

category 5 UTP data cable

_____
_____
_____
_____

CDPD

_____
_____
_____
_____

cell

_____
_____
_____
_____

cell site

_____
_____
_____
_____

Cisco Works 2000

_____
_____
_____
_____

client

_____
_____
_____
_____

coaxial cable

_____
_____
_____
_____

data rates

_____
_____

dual-band

E1

electromagnetic interference (EMI)

electromagnetic spectrum

Ethernet

FCC

fiber-optic cable

firmware

_____
_____
_____
_____

FM

_____
_____
_____
_____

foil twisted pair

_____
_____
_____
_____

frequency

_____
_____
_____
_____

frequency reuse

_____
_____
_____
_____

high availability

_____
_____
_____
_____

interference

_____
_____
_____
_____

GHz

_____
_____

ground

IEEE

IMT-2000

ISP

key rotation

LAN

line of sight

link

_____
_____
_____
_____

LMDS

_____
_____
_____
_____

MDS

_____
_____
_____
_____

microwave

_____
_____
_____
_____

MMDS

_____
_____
_____
_____

MTSO

_____
_____
_____
_____

OFDM

_____
_____
_____
_____

open architecture

_____
_____

OSI model

packet

PCS

physical layer

power

power save mode

presentation layer

QoS

_____
_____
_____
_____

radio

_____
_____
_____
_____

receiver

_____
_____
_____
_____

refraction

_____
_____
_____
_____

RF

_____
_____
_____
_____

scalability

_____
_____
_____

ScTP

_____
_____
_____
_____

spread spectrum

_____
_____
_____
_____

STP

_____
_____
_____
_____

TCP

_____
_____
_____
_____

third generation (3G)

_____
_____
_____
_____

throughput

_____
_____
_____
_____

total cost of ownership (TCO)

_____
_____
_____
_____

transmitter

_____
_____
_____
_____

UMTS

_____
_____
_____
_____

U-NII

_____
_____

_____
_____

UTP cable

_____
_____
_____
_____

vertical market

_____
_____
_____
_____

virtual private network (VPN)

_____
_____
_____
_____

wired equivalent privacy (WEP)

_____
_____
_____
_____

WLAN

_____
_____
_____
_____

Focus Questions

1. What is one potential advantage of 802.11 wireless technology over WAN links for connecting buildings on a campus?

    _____
    _____
    _____
    _____

2. Why would someone use STP?

    _____
    _____

3.   What are two methods of performing building-to-building connection
        using wired media or optical fiber?

        _____
        _____
        _____
        _____

4.   How must you route a cable to a wireless access point if the intended route
        passes through a wall that is designated as a firewall?

        _____
        _____
        _____
        _____

5.   If you want to configure a wireless network to connect two buildings, will
        the existing rubber-duckie antennas be adequate?

        _____
        _____
        _____
        _____

6.   What is the purpose of a government-issued license for microwave radio
        links?

        _____
        _____
        _____
        _____

7.   What is the U.S. Government agency that controls the use of radio
        frequencies?

        _____
        _____
        _____
        _____

8.   The 2.4-GHz frequency range used for 802.11b Wi-Fi equipment is in
        which frequency band?

        _____
        _____
        _____
        _____

9.　The 5.0-GHz frequency range used for 802.11a Wi-Fi equipment is in which frequency band?

_____

_____

_____

_____

10.　What frequency band does 802.11g use?

_____

_____

_____

_____

11.　What is meant by frequency reuse?

_____

_____

_____

_____

12.　What is the station called that cell phones communicate with?

_____

_____

_____

_____

13.　What is the name of the period of time when one cell phone or wireless client access device is transferring communications from one base station or access point to another?

_____

_____

_____

_____

14.　What is the most recent version of cell phone technology called?

_____

_____

_____

_____

15.　What is the role of client adapter equipment?

_____

_____

_____

_____

16.   What do access points do?

_____
_____
_____
_____

17.   What is a dual-band access point?

_____
_____
_____
_____

18.   What is the potential for interference in networks that use 802.11x
        technologies?

_____
_____
_____
_____

19.   What can you do to avoid interference while using 802.11 wireless
        equipment?

_____
_____
_____
_____

20.   What is an advantage of using products from a single vendor for all your
        802.11 networking?

_____
_____
_____
_____

21.   What are some of the consumer products that use embedded wireless
        technology?

_____
_____
_____

22.   What are some advantages of using WLAN technologies in an office
        environment?

_____
_____
_____
_____

23. What are some of the vertical markets that are adopting WLAN technology?

_____

_____

_____

_____

24. What is the difference UTP and STP cabling?

_____

_____

_____

_____

25. What are some advantages of using UTP cabling?

_____

_____

_____

_____

26. What are some disadvantages of using UTP cabling?

_____

_____

_____

_____

27. Aside from WLANs, what are some of the types of wireless communications in use today?

_____

_____

_____

_____

Review Questions

1. *Thinnet*, *Thicknet*, and *Cheapernet* all refer to which pre-802.11 media that is still popular for the transmission of video?
   A. UTP
   B. STP
   C. Optical fiber
   D. Coaxial cable

2. What is it called when signals from one pair of wires in a cable appear in a different pair?
   A. Cross talk
   B. Mutual cross inductance

C.   UTP
D.   Signal leakage

3.   Which of the following is *not* an advantage of wireless technology?
A.   Mobility
B.   Scalability
C.   Flexibility
D.   Short- and long-term cost savings
E.   No need for wired infrastructure
F.   Reliability in harsh environments
G.   Reduced installation time

4.   Starting with the most intimate and ending with the most global, order the following types of network: personal-area network (PAN), local-area network (LAN), wide-area network (WAN), and metropolitan-area network (MAN).
A.   PAN, MAN, LAN, WAN
B.   WAN, MAN, PAN, LAN
C.   PAN, LAN, MAN, WAN
D.   WAN, PAN, LAN, MAN

5.   Which of the following groups use primarily wireless technology?
A.   Television, AM/FM radio, satellite TV
B.   Bluetooth, Wi-Fi, microwave ovens
C.   Microwave ovens, Global Positioning Satellites (GPS), cellular phones
D.   CB radios, cordless phones weather radios
E.   A, C, and D
F.   All of the above

6.   Which of the following devices may cause interference in a wireless network?
A.   Cordless telephone
B.   Television
C.   Microwave oven
D.   A and C
E.   All of the above

7.   Which of the following are used in Layer 1 of the OSI model?
A.   Twisted-pair cable
B.   Coaxial cable
C.   Fiber-optic cable
D.   Propagated radio waves
E.   A, B, and C
F.   All of the above

Notes

Chapter 2

IEEE 802.11 and Network Interface Cards

Installing an Institute of Electrical and Electronics Engineers (IEEE) 802.11-based network requires an understanding of the building blocks.

It is critical that you understand wireless standards. First, realize that standards come in two forms: de jure standards, which have the force of law or are recognized by standards authorities; and de facto, which are standards that the marketplace accepts regardless of their standardization.

The 802.11 standard has grown into a family of standards:
- The original 802.11 describes a 2-Mbps standard operating in the 2.4-GHz segment of the Industrial Scientific Medical band.
- 802.11b describes a 5- or 11-Mbps system that operates in the same band and largely supercedes the original, although older installations can share the band.
- 802.11a describes a 55-Mbps system that operates in the 5-GHz band.
- 802.1g drafted standard uses the orthogonal frequency division multiplex modulation system of 802.11a to operate up to a speed of 54 Mbps in the 2.4-GHz spectrum.

The physical layer PHY for radio communications is intangible, but rules for collision avoidance must exist. It is also important to distinguish between an infrastructure network—that is, one in which an access point (AP) that is attached to a larger network communicates with all units but not station (STA) to station—and an ad hoc network, in which every STA connects to all others. The smallest wireless network, or microcell, is called a *basic system set*. Multiple basic system sets can be chained together to create an extended service set (ESS). Switching from one basic system set to another as one moves about is called "roaming."

The best way to determine where to place various elements of a wireless network is to perform a site survey. Field strength measurements can be taken to determine if coverage from various access points is adequate.

Concept Questions

1. What is meant by the terms *acknowledged connection-oriented* and *connectionless service*?

    _____

    _____

    _____

    _____

    _____

2. Why is FHSS a superior method of encoding wireless messages?

_____

_____

_____

_____

_____

3. What is the Industrial Scientific Medical radio band that 802.11a and 802.11g operate on?

_____

_____

_____

_____

_____

4. Why is interoperability important between the various PC card wireless network interface cards that clients plug into laptops and other devices?

_____

_____

_____

_____

5. Every network application is a unique installation. Before you install the system, you should use the Site Survey tool to determine the optimum placement of networking components. What operating and environmental conditions should you consider when performing a site survey to maximize range, coverage, and network performance?

_____

_____

_____

_____

6. What are some benefits of standardization?

_____

_____

_____

_____

_____

Vocabulary Exercise

access control

_____

_____

ACK

ACU

ANSI

associated

bandwidth

basic service set (BSS)

biphase shift keying (BPSK)

bit rate

_____
_____
_____
_____

Bluetooth

_____
_____
_____
_____

BSM

_____
_____
_____
_____

CCITT

_____
_____
_____
_____

CCK

_____
_____
_____
_____

CCO

_____
_____
_____
_____

channel

_____
_____
_____
_____

clear channel assessment (CCA)

_____
_____

client adapter

complementary code keying (CCK)

confidentiality

CRC

CTS

data link layer

data integrity

DCF

_____
_____
_____
_____

de facto standards

_____
_____
_____
_____

de jure standards

_____
_____
_____
_____

differential quadrature phase shift keying (DQPSK)

_____
_____
_____
_____

DIFS

_____
_____
_____
_____

distributed coordination function

_____
_____
_____
_____

DS

_____
_____
_____
_____

EIFS

_____
_____

ESS

ETSI

FCS

frequency hopping spread spectrum (FHSS)

free space

free space loss

frequency hopping

GHz

_____
_____
_____
_____

GUI

_____
_____
_____
_____

IEEE

_____
_____
_____
_____

IETF

_____
_____
_____
_____

IFS

_____
_____
_____
_____

Industrial Scientific Medical band

_____
_____
_____
_____

infrared

_____
_____
_____
_____

interoperability

_____
_____

IrDA

ISO

ITU

KHz

light emitting diodes (LEDs)

LLC

LSDU

LSM

_____
_____
_____
_____

MAC address

_____
_____
_____
_____

MAN

_____
_____
_____
_____

microcell

_____
_____
_____
_____

modulation

_____
_____
_____
_____

MPDU

_____
_____
_____
_____

MSDU

_____
_____
_____
_____

multicast

_____
_____

NAV

NIC

orthogonal frequency division multiplexing (OFDM)

PC card

PCF

PCMCIA card (PC card)

peer-to-peer network

34

PIFS

_____
_____
_____
_____

PLCP

_____
_____
_____
_____

PMD

_____
_____
_____
_____

PnP

_____
_____
_____
_____

propagation

_____
_____
_____
_____

protocol

_____
_____
_____
_____

PSK

_____
_____
_____
_____

quadruple phase Shift keying

_____
_____

range

RISC processor

roaming

RTS

SFD

SIFS

site survey

spectrum

_____

_____

_____

_____

SSID

_____

_____

_____

_____

STA

_____

_____

_____

_____

status

_____

_____

_____

_____

Focus Questions

1.   What did the term *WECA* signify?

_____

_____

_____

_____

2.   What does Wi-Fi stand for? Explain its significance.

_____

_____

_____

_____

3.   What are the frequency assignments for each of the versions of 802.11 wireless networks?

_____

_____

_____

_____

_____

4. Is the IEEE a federal agency chartered to ensure the adherence to wireless standards? Explain.

_____

_____

_____

_____

_____

5. What role does the PHY layer play in Wi-Fi and IR communications?

_____

_____

_____

_____

6. What is the official name and purpose of the IEEE 802.11 standard for Wi-Fi?

_____

_____

_____

_____

_____

7. Some wireless network interface cards that plug into laptops come in a format called PC card. What is meant by that?

_____

_____

_____

_____

_____

8. What is the difference between a MAC and a STA?

_____

_____

_____

9. What is another term for a STA moving from one AP to another AP?

_____

_____

_____

38

10.   Must every STA remain in constant radio contact with every other STA? Justify your answer.

_____
_____
_____
_____

11.   In IEEE 802.11, do mobile and portable mean the same thing? Justify your answer.

_____
_____
_____
_____

12.   What is the smallest unit of coverage for a WLAN?

_____
_____
_____
_____

13.   What happens to data rates as a station moves farther from its AP?

_____
_____
_____
_____

14.   If the frame check sequence (FCS) of the received frame is correct, the receiving station usually responds with an ACK frame acknowledgment. Lack of reception of an expected ACK frame indicates to the source station that an error has occurred. What is this transmission technique called?

_____
_____
_____
_____

15.   What defines the characteristics of, as well as the method of transmitting and receiving data through, a wireless medium between two or more STAs that use the same PHY system?

_____
_____
_____
_____

16. How many channels of the 2.4-GHz band does the Federal Communications Commission (FCC) authorize for Wi-Fi operation in the U.S.?

_____
_____
_____
_____

17. What term describes the series of overlapping or half-overlapping channels in a given spectrum allocation?

_____
_____
_____
_____

18. The IEEE 802.11a standard provides speeds up to 54 Mbps through OFDM. This technique uses multiple subcarriers spaced 312.5 KHz apart. Each subcarrier carries a portion of the user data, and four subcarriers are used as pilots. How many carriers actually move information?

_____
_____
_____
_____

19. What was the data rate of the original 802.11 systems?

_____
_____
_____
_____

20. What information is found on the Status page of the Aironet Client utility?

_____
_____
_____
_____

21. What information is found on the Statistics page of the Aironet Client utility?

_____
_____
_____
_____

Review Questions

1. Which of the following is not an advantage of standardization?
   A. Interoperability among multiple vendors' products
   B. Quicker obsolescence
   C. Faster product development
   D. Stability
   E. Ability to upgrade
   F. Cost reductions

2. What is the role of IEEE in WLAN activities?
   A. Monitor frequencies and police interference
   B. Determine which vendors earn Wi-Fi logo certification
   C. Promote and update the 802.11 standard and its versions
   D. Lobby government agencies for increased funding

3. Which of the following is the least accurate statement?
   A. In infrastructure mode, all stations in the BSS communicate via the AP; stations do not communicate directly.
   B. A BSS has one service set ID (SSID).
   C. In an independent basic service set (IBSS), IEEE 802.11 stations communicate directly.
   D. Because they are often formed without preplanning and exist for only as long as the WLAN is needed, IBSS networks are often referred to as ad hoc networks.
   E. An extended service set may be built from multiple BSSs.
   F. A common distribution system can connect multiple BSS and IBSS, and it must be wireless.

4. Which of the following is the biggest disadvantage of 802.11a?
   A. It uses the 5-GHz frequency band, instead of 2.4 GHz, precluding backward compatibility.
   B. It uses specialized connectors so that appropriate antennas and transmitters will always be matched.
   C. Dual band equipment will allow operation in both bands.
   D. 802.11g uses the same modulation method but operates on the 2.4-GHz band.

5. Which of the following is not an advantage of the IR PHY standard?
   A. Infrared radiation does not pass through walls and is significantly attenuated passing through exterior windows, limiting the potential for eavesdropping.
   B. It has a range of only about 20 meters maximum.
   C. It will operate only in indoor environments.
   D. Worldwide, there are currently no frequency allocation or bandwidth allocation regulatory restrictions on infrared emissions.

Notes

Chapter 3

Wireless Radio Technology

Wireless local-area network (WLAN) technology rests on more than 100 years of patient effort by thousands of dedicated researchers. The techniques used in 802.11x receivers and transmitters are extremely advanced, wrestling more bandwidth and range out of the available frequencies than ever was imagined just a few decades ago. Wireless technology is built on certain principals of physics, and the language used to describe them involves mathematics. The waves of radio, either low frequency for AM or microwave such as 802.11 and the links to the space shuttle, all follow the same laws. Fortunately, understanding that the decibel is merely a ratio of the power of one device versus the power of another one makes it easy to understand the rest.

Some frequencies require protection from interference. These are called licensed frequencies, and permission is required to use them. Certain unlicensed bands, the Industrial, Science, Medical among them, are the spectrum in which Wi-Fi operates.

Radio waves move energy across large distances, but the really interesting things happen when they encounter obstructions or other waves. If the obstructions are large with respect to an individual wave, the waves are likely to reflect. If, on the other hand, the surface is smooth compared to the size of a wave, radio waves can often travel around the obstruction and continue on the other side. When a radio wave meets another, or even its own reflection, the result can be a null, where the waves are out of phase (and then add up and cancel), or a peak, where two waves meet in phase and reinforce each other. A technique called *diversity antennas* improves system performance by spacing antennas in such as way that both cannot be in nulls and that at least one is getting a good signal.

You can place information on radio waves by modulating the waves. Analog modulation systems change the shape of the wave to represent the signal to be transmitted. Digital systems work by causing changes in the radio signals that reflect the 1s and 0s being transmitted. By and large, digital radio systems offer superior performance and have taken over from analog systems, such as AM and FM radio and conventional (not HDTV) television.

Concept Questions

1. Describe four basic properties of a sine wave. How is such a wave used to carry information?

_____
_____
_____
_____

_____

_____

_____

_____

_____

_____

2. The formula for calculating decibels is dB = 10 log10 (Pfinal/Pref): where dB = The amount of decibels. This usually represents a loss in power.

Pref = The reference power. This is the original power.

Pfinal = The final power. This is the delivered power after some process has occurred.

This formula calculates either a loss or a gain, but usually it measures loss. What is a simple rule by which to estimate the amount of loss or gain for radio frequency (RF) power?

_____

_____

_____

_____

_____

3. Which is likely to be larger: digital bandwidth or throughput? Justify your answer.

_____

_____

_____

_____

_____

4. What is the effect of a radio wave reflecting back onto itself 180 degrees out of phase with itself?

_____

_____

_____

_____

_____

5. How is it that IEEE 802.11b and 802.11g operate in the same 2.4-GHz frequency band, but one only carries 11 Mbps and the other carries 54 Mbps?

_____

_____

_____

_____

_____

6. Describe the steps involved in the process of analog-to-digital (A to D) conversion.

_____
_____
_____
_____
_____

7. List and give a short description of four properties of electromagnetic waves.

_____
_____
_____
_____
_____

Vocabulary Exercise

802.11x

_____
_____
_____
_____

access point

_____
_____
_____
_____

ad hoc mode

_____
_____
_____
_____

amplitude

_____
_____
_____
_____

audio amplifier

_____
_____

antenna gain

attenuation

bandwidth

BSPK

carrier frequency

carrier wave

complementary code keying (CCK)

code division multiple access (CDMA)

_____
_____
_____
_____

carrier sense multiple access collision avoidance (CSMA/CA)

_____
_____
_____
_____

carrier sense multiple access collision detect (CSMA/CD)

_____
_____
_____
_____

compression

_____
_____
_____
_____

dB

_____
_____
_____
_____

dBd

_____
_____
_____
_____

dBi

_____
_____
_____
_____

dBm

_____
_____

demodulation

diffraction

diversity antenna

dwell time

DSSS

EIRP

EM

frequency

_____
_____
_____
_____

frequency hopping

_____
_____
_____
_____

frequency hopping spread spectrum (FHSS)

_____
_____
_____
_____

frequency division multiple access (FDMA)

_____
_____
_____
_____

FSK

_____
_____
_____
_____

Gaussian noise

_____
_____
_____
_____

Hz

_____
_____
_____
_____

intermediate frequency (IF)

_____
_____

ISM

multipath

noise

path loss

polarization

range

reflection

refraction

_____
_____
_____
_____

RF amplifier

_____
_____
_____
_____

Shannon, Claude

_____
_____
_____
_____

speed of light (c)

_____
_____
_____
_____

time division multiplex access (TDMA)

_____
_____
_____
_____

unlicensed spectrum

_____
_____
_____
_____

Focus Questions

1. Does a radio wave travel through air or space by displacing or pushing out of its way the particles that are in front of it?

_____
_____

2. What makes the sine wave unusual among waves?

_____
_____

3.   In what unit is frequency measured?

_____
_____
_____

4.   What is the frequency of common household utility AC current?

_____
_____

5.   Name the process of recovering information from a modulated carrier wave.

_____
_____

6.   What is the effect of applying DC voltage to a specially ground crystal?

_____
_____
_____

7.   When two sine waves differ by any amount besides 0 and 360 degrees, they are said to be out of phase. If the two waves come together at 0 or 360 degrees, they tend to add together. What happens if the two waves come together at 180 degrees out of phase?

_____
_____
_____

8.   In WLANs, power levels as low as one milliwatt (mW) or one one-thousandth (1/1000th) of a watt can be used for a small area. What is the maximum power that can be used on the 2.4-GHz band in the United States?

_____
_____
_____

9.   The Bel is a large unit of sound named for Alexander Graham Bell. What is the term for one-tenth of a Bel?

_____
_____

10.   What does the following formula tell you about the relationship between frequency and wavelength?
        $c = \lambda * f$, where c = the speed of light ($3 * 10^5$ m/s)

_____
_____

11.   Why is the electromagnetic spectrum a finite resource?

_____

_____

_____

_____

12.   What is the European version of the US Federal Communications Commission that regulates spectrum use?

_____

_____

13.   What is required before operating a radio device in a licensed band such as AM and FM radio, aviation bands, ham, or short-wave radio?

_____

_____

_____

14.   Generally speaking, what part of the electromagnetic spectrum is considered to be useable for radio or microwave?

_____

_____

15.   What device can you use to display the shape of a waveform over time?

_____

_____

16.   What is a simple word to describe unwanted energy being added to a message-carrying signal?

_____

_____

17.   Estimate how long will it take to transmit a 4MB file over a T1 (1.544 Mbps) link (ignoring overhead and line failures)?

_____

_____

_____

_____

18.   Why are channel sets used?

_____

_____

_____

19.   _____ or _____ noise affects all bands equally. _____
       _____ can interfere with one channel and leave an adjacent

channel unaffected. Which one can possibly be avoided by simply changing channels?

___

20.   What was the data rate of the original 802.11 systems?

___

Review Questions

1.   Which of the following is least likely to be an important use of radio in the home?
        A.   AM and FM radio broadcasts
        B.   Cordless phones
        C.   Garage door openers
        D.   Wireless networks
        E.   Radio-controlled toys
        G.   One-way and two-way satellite communications
        H.   Television remote control units
        I.   Cell phones

2.   A dB has no particular defined reference and can refer to any change of power. In measurements where the same reference is used to compare many things, the reference value is usually written after the dB. What is the symbol for dB with reference to hypothetically perfect antenna?
        A.   dB milliwatt (dBm)
        B.   dB dipole (dBd)
        C.   dB isotropic (dBi)
        D.   dB undefined reference (dBx)

3.   The electromagnetic (EM) spectrum is simply a name that scientists have given to the set of all types of radiation, when discussed as a group. Which of the following is *not* an example of radiation in the electromagnetic (EM) spectrum? (Choose two.)
        A.   The visible light that comes from a lamp
        B.   Radio that come from a radio or TV station
        C.   Music that comes from a CD player
        D.   Microwaves inside a microwave oven
        E.   Infrared light from a TV remote control
        F.   Wind
        G.   Ultraviolet light (UV) from a special florescent tube
        H.   X-rays from a mammography machine
        I.   Gamma rays from space

4.   Which of the following is a valid frequency for Wi-Fi? Choose all that apply.
        A.   902–938 MHz (US ISM Band)
        B.   2.4–2.4835 GHz (US ISM Band)

C.   5.725 GHz–5.850 GHz
D.   789.2500–793.7500

5.   Correctly order the following steps of the A to D process.
      1) Assign a discrete value to each sample.
      2) Sample analog wave amplitudes at specific instances in time.
      3) Convert each discrete value to a stream of bits.
      4) Transmit or store the stream of bits as required by the application.
      A.   1-2-3-4
      B.   2-1-4-3
      C.   1-4-3-2
      D.   2-1-3-4

6.   What does the description "A disturbance or variation that transfers energy progressively from point to point in a medium" define?
      A.   Amplitude
      B.   A wave
      C.   Frequency
      D.   Electromagnetic spectrum

7.   Correctly order the following types of electromagnetic waves in order of increasing frequency and energy, and decreasing wavelength.
      1) Radio waves
      2) Visible light
      3) Infrared light
      4) Microwaves
      A.   1-2-3-4
      B.   2-1-4-3
      C.   1-4-3-2
      D.   2-1-3-4

Notes

Chapter 4

Wireless Topologies

The move to wireless local-area network (WLAN) technology has created a new efficiency for business users of computers. No longer are workers confined to a single place to do work; they can synchronize their laptops and run to a conference room without ever touching a desk they call their own. To facilitate this, many laptops now ship with wireless network interface cards built in.

The topologies of wireless technology center around two network layouts. First is the ad hoc network, in which all clients can communicate with all others. Second is the infrastructure network, in which all clients communicate with an access point (AP), which acts as a hub and relay.

The area served by an AP is called a basic service set. These sets can be joined by wired or wireless means to form an extended service set. If the connection is wireless, the connecting device is functioning as a wireless bridge. Another form of bridge is called the workgroup bridge. Its function is to join to the network those units that do not have wireless network interface cards of their own.

The frequencies on which networked devices broadcast are determined according to a scheme that the system designer works out. The goal is to provide complete coverage while minimizing overlap.

The antenna that is chosen largely determines the shape of the wireless cells. Although most APs have a dipole antenna built in, most also have the capability of connecting to an external antenna to shape the area of coverage and to extend range. The connectors that are used to couple to these external antennas are proprietary to manufacturers. Cisco uses a reverse polarity TNC connector.

Some items of network equipment can back up for others. Two APs, for instance, can provide load balancing or hot standby services for each other.

Concept Questions

1.   Why would anyone want to install a wireless system on top of an existing wired network?

_____
_____
_____
_____
_____

2.   What are some operating systems that are commonly used in handheld computers?

_____
_____

_____
_____
_____
_____

3. Can 802.11 products carry voice communications as well as data? Justify your answer.

_____
_____
_____
_____
_____

4. What types of drivers are available for Cisco wireless client adapters?

_____
_____
_____
_____
_____

5. What is the function of a wireless bridge?

_____
_____
_____
_____
_____

6. What layers make up the Cisco three-layer hierarchical model?

_____
_____
_____
_____
_____

7. Describe modularity and list two benefits of using modularity when designing a network.

_____
_____
_____
_____
_____

8. Describe redundancy and explain how it is beneficial in a WLAN environment.

_____
_____

9.   Describe scalability and explain how it is beneficial in a WLAN environment.

Vocabulary Exercise

access layer

architecture for voice, video, and integrated data (AVVID)

API

application layer

authentication

AVVID

backbone

base station

basic service set (BSS)

beacon

core layer

coverage area

DHCP

distribution layer

extended service set

firewall

infrastructure

ISL

LANE

mast mount antenna

microcell

modem

multirate shifting

NDIS

omni-directional

parabolic dish

Peer-to-Peer (Ad Hoc) Topology (IBSS)

pico cell

point-to-multipoint

_____
_____
_____
_____

point-to-point

_____
_____
_____
_____

probe request

_____
_____
_____
_____

probe response

_____
_____
_____
_____

receiver sensitivity

_____
_____
_____
_____

Reverse-Polarity-TNC (RP-TNC) connector

_____
_____
_____
_____

SoHo

_____
_____
_____
_____

TNC

_____
_____

_____

transmit power

_____

wireless repeater

_____

WLAN topology

_____

workgroup bridge

_____

Yagi

_____

Focus Questions

1.   The main difference between desktops and laptops is that components in a laptop are smaller. Similarly, palm top computers, personal digital assistants (PDAs), and other small computing devices are assuming part of the role filled by laptops. Which of these devices can be equipped with wireless technology?

_____

2.   What is a strong advantage of wireless network interface cards?

_____

_____

_____

_____

3.   Desktop computers have expansion slots. What do laptop computers have?

_____

4.   Desktop PCs and laptops perform functions that can be associated with all seven layers of the OSI reference model. The TCP/IP protocol defines a single layer, referred to as the process layer or the application layer, for the functionality associated with which OSI layers?

_____

_____

_____

5.   What is an advantage of handheld computers over most laptops or notebooks?

_____

_____

_____

_____

6.   What are some operating systems that are commonly used in handheld computers?

_____

_____

_____

_____

7.   Can 802.11 products carry voice communications as well as data? Explain your answer.

_____

_____

_____

_____

8.   The Cisco Aironet wireless radio modules provide transparent data communications among fixed, portable, or mobile wireless devices; other devices—both wireless and wired—are fully compatible with devices that support plug-and-play (PnP) technology, such as laptops, desktops, and mobile computing devices. The primary function of the client adapters is to transfer data packets transparently through the wireless infrastructure. By what other names are these devices known as?

_____
_____
_____
_____

9.   The WLAN adaptors operate similarly to a standard network adapter, except that the cable has been replaced by a radio connection. At what layers of the OSI reference model do they operate?

_____
_____
_____
_____

10.   What is inline power injection?

_____
_____
_____
_____

11.   If you need to extend the area served by a wireless network, what device do you need?

_____
_____

12.   What is the function of a workgroup bridge?

_____
_____
_____
_____

13.   Can a workgroup bridge be used in a peer-to-peer network? Justify your answer.

_____
_____
_____
_____

14.   How can a workgroup bridge provide individual Media Access Control (MAC) addresses for the network devices it connects to and AP?

_____
_____
_____

15.   What kind of connector is on the antenna wire extending from Cisco Aironet products? What does it do?

_____
_____

16.   What is the maximum range that can be anticipated if you are using an extremely high-gain antenna such as the solid dish?

_____

_____

17.   At which layer of the OSI reference model do antennas operate?

_____

_____

18.   A network engineer installs wireless bridges in two campus buildings and points their directional antennas toward the main building, where an omni directional antenna is installed. What must he do to allow the systems to interconnect?

_____

_____

_____

_____

19.   A hot standby system provides redundancy but no load sharing. A load balancing system splits the load between two access points based on what parameters?

_____

_____

_____

_____

20.   When a client comes online, it broadcasts a probe request. An AP that hears this will respond with information about the AP, such as RF hops to the backbone, load, and so on. APs also broadcast similar information at predetermined and programmable intervals. What are these broadcasts called?

_____

_____

21.   What is the function of the access layer in the Cisco three-layer hierarchical model?

_____

_____

_____

_____

22.   What is the function of the distribution layer in the Cisco three-layer hierarchical model?

_____

_____

_____

23.   What is the function of the core layer in the Cisco three-layer hierarchical model?

_____
_____
_____
_____

24.   In a base station-DSL WLAN topology, why is access to the wired network not available to the base station?

_____
_____
_____
_____

25.   What is the difference between a basic infrastructure topology (BSS) and an extended infrastructure topology (ESS) WLAN topology?

_____
_____
_____
_____

26.   What are some common reasons that a company might implement VLANs?

_____
_____
_____
_____

Review Questions

1.   How does an increase in user mobility result in an increase in productivity? (Choose three.)
        A.   It can require workers to stay home to save on office rentals.
        B.   Users can be connected to corporate files and resources while they are in the meeting.
        C.   There is less personal preparation copying files; users can simply pick up and go, with all of their resources available.
        D.   Instant messaging, e-mail, printing, files, and Internet access are all easily accessible.

2.   Which of the following is not a commonly available user interface for handheld computers?
        A.   Keyboards
        B.   Touch screens

  C. Pen or stylus
  D. Voice activated
  E. Fully functional operating system
  F. Scanners

3. Which of the following is a consideration for choosing mobile devices for integration into your WLAN?
  A. Using only 802.11-compliant devices to communicate with the rest of your equipment
  B. Choosing software application packages that will be compatible with the devices used in your particular environment
  C. Battery life and durability suitable to your application
  D. Presence of AC power near all APs

4. You should carefully choose antennas to provide optimum coverage for the installation without offering opportunities for interference or snooping. Which of the following is not an important distinction among antennas?
  A. Gain and range
  B. Type and length of mounting screws
  C. Form factors and mounting method
  D. Beam widths

5. Many corporations are supplying their workforce with laptops instead of desktop models. While workers are in the office, the laptop is typically connected to a docking station with a large display monitor, full-size keyboard, and a mouse for improved ergonomic use. Which of the following is not an advantage of this approach?
  A. The laptop is easily transported for business or personal use, at home or on the road.
  B. Laptops and docking stations limit the need to purchase and maintain two devices for each employee.
  C. Laptops and docking stations eliminate the need to constantly transfer files between two PCs.
  D. Laptop hard drives contain sensitive corporate data.

Notes

Chapter 5

Access Points

An access point (AP) is the communications gateway between various wireless clients and the wired or wireless network. As such, an AP can be considered a wireless hub. It also, however, can function as a repeater, extending the range of a network, and as a wireless bridge, joining portions of a network.

To configure a network, first gather the required information:
- The intended system name
- The wireless service set identifier (SSID) for the radio network
- A unique IP address for the AP (if not connected to a DHCP server)
- A default gateway address and subnet mask (if the AP is not on the same subnet as the PC)
- The Simple Network Management Protocol (SNMP) community name and the SNMP file attribute (if SNMP is in use)
- The Media Access Control (MAC) address from the label on the bottom of the AP, if IPSU is in use

Power up the AP by paying close attention to the instructions regarding cabling. Some APs take their power feed from the Ethernet cable and require special power injection adapters or switches. A light emitting diode (LED) sequence indicates boot, and a green LED indicates normal operation.

Configuration can take place using a Web interface and a browser, a Telnet connection and a command line, or a console connection. Configuration parameters deal with setting up the Ethernet connection, as well as setting up various parameters for the radio module.

Concept Questions

1. An inline power system feeds power to certain APs over the Ethernet port. What is its operating voltage? Is an electrician usually required to perform these installations? Do the "rules of cabling" still apply? Justify your answer.

_____

_____

_____

_____

_____

_____

2. What are some basic precautions to follow when connecting an AP?

_____

_____

_____
_____
_____

3.   What is the advantage of using the Auto setting on the Ethernet Hardware page?

_____
_____
_____
_____
_____

4.   Why are there receive and transmit antenna controls on the Radio Port hardware setup page?

_____
_____
_____
_____
_____

5.   Why would you want to lower the transmit power using the Transmit Power control on the Port hardware page?

_____
_____
_____
_____
_____

Vocabulary Exercise

Aironet

_____
_____
_____
_____

ARP

_____
_____
_____

ASCII

_____
_____

authorization

Beacon Period (Kµs)

BOOTP

CDP

CLI

data retries

default gateway

74

DHCP server

_____
_____
_____
_____

diversity

_____
_____
_____
_____

DNS

_____
_____
_____
_____

DTIM

_____
_____
_____
_____

file server

_____
_____
_____
_____

FTP

_____
_____
_____
_____

gateway

_____
_____
_____
_____

hot standby

_____
_____

HTTP

Internet Protocol (IP) address

IP subnet mask

IPSU

load balancing

multicast

protocol filters

service set identifier (SSID)

_____

_____

_____

_____

signal strength

_____

_____

_____

_____

SNMP

_____

_____

_____

_____

SNTP

_____

_____

_____

_____

standby assignment

_____

_____

_____

_____

Telnet

_____

_____

_____

_____

TFTP

_____

_____

_____

_____

unicast

_____

_____

Focus Questions

1. Frequency regulation varies slightly around the world. What function allows a visitor from a foreign country to compensate for the frequencies found locally?

   _____

   _____

2. What feature provides uninterrupted network connectivity by allowing an AP to act as a backup for another AP?

   _____

   _____

   _____

   _____

3. What does a protocol filter do?

   _____

   _____

   _____

   _____

4. What are some options for the control and configuration of APs?

   _____

   _____

   _____

   _____

5. Can an AP serve for both the 802.11a and 802.11b standards?

   _____

   _____

6. If an AP is configured via Telnet or a Web interface, where does it get its IP address?

   _____

   _____

   _____

   _____

7. What do the lights on an AP show?

   _____

   _____

   _____

   _____

8. When you are configuring an AP via a console connection, what HyperTerminal settings should you use?

_____

_____

_____

_____

_____

9. Is the SSID case sensitive?

_____

_____

10. If DHCP does not supply the IP subnet mask, what will be the default?

_____

_____

11. What is the default Web page for the Cisco Aironet 1100 and 1200 series?

_____

_____

_____

_____

12. What display indicates that an AP is starting up?

_____

_____

_____

_____

13. Can a workgroup bridge be used in a peer-to-peer network? Justify your answer.

_____

_____

_____

_____

14. On what page would you set MAC address filtering?

_____

_____

15. Why would you set protocol filters on an AP?

_____

_____

_____

_____

_____

79

16. What is the SSID? How many characters can it be in length?

_____

_____

_____

_____

17. If "Allow Broadcast SSID to Associate?" on the Broadcast Port Hardware page is set to "No," what happens when an AP hears signals from users from a neighboring network?

_____

_____

_____

_____

18. What is the purpose of the Name Server Setup page?

_____

_____

_____

_____

19. A hot standby system provides redundancy but no load sharing. A load balancing system splits the load between two APs based on what parameters?

_____

_____

_____

20. What is the meaning of entering "Basic" in the Radio Part Hardware Data Rate settings boxes?

_____

_____

_____

_____

21. What are some of the important features of an access point? (List at least four.)

_____

_____

_____

_____

22. What two basic GUI interfaces are available on Cisco access points (depending on the AP image)?

_____

_____

_____

_____

80

23. What two pieces of numerical information identify devices on the network?

24. What four IOS commands can be used to check the status of an interface on the access point?

25. List and give the description of at least four options that can be used with the **debug dot11 dot11radio** privileged EXEC command.

26. What are the two steps involved in the process of configuring QoS on a Cisco access point?

Review Questions

1. Load balancing on an AP is set to automatically direct client devices to an AP that provides the best connection to the network. Which of the following features can be used to set load balancing? (Choose three.)
   A. Number of users
   B. Height above average terrain
   C. Bit error rates
   D. Signal strength

2. Which of the following are not roles of wireless APs?
   A. An AP can link wired and wireless networks.
   B. An AP can protect network users against electromagnetic interference (EMI) and radio frequency interface (RFI).
   C. Multiple APs can be configured to allow wireless users to roam without interruption.
   D. An AP can provide security.
   E. An AP can act as a wireless repeater or extension point for the wireless network.

3. Before you set up an AP, what information should you gather? (Select the best six answers.)
   A. The intended system name
   B. The wireless SSID for the radio network
   C. A unique IP address for the AP (if not connected to a DHCP server)
   D. The address of the building and its height above average terrain (HAAT)
   E. A default gateway address and subnet mask (if the AP is not on the same subnet as the PC)
   F. The department manager's name and e-mail address
   G. The Simple Network Management Protocol (SNMP) community name and the SNMP file attribute (if SNMP is in use)
   H. The MAC address from the label on the bottom of the AP, if the IP Setup Utility (IPSU) is in use
   I. The effective radiated power of all sources of interference

4. List some of the items that you can configure on an AP Ethernet port. (Choose all that are appropriate.)
   A. Key configuration and statistical information for the Ethernet port on the AP (Ethernet Port)
   B. Basic identity information for the Ethernet port (Ethernet identification)
   C. Ethernet port connection speed (Ethernet hardware)
   D. Antenna power-matching adjustments (Ethernet antenna)
   E. Settings for protocol filters (Ethernet filters)
   F. Operational status information for the Ethernet port (Ethernet advanced)
   G. Form fields to make temporary changes in port status for troubleshooting purposes (Ethernet advanced)
   H. Gain and range

5. What are three classes of filters that can be set using the Ethernet Protocol Filters page?
   A. EtherType (IP, ARP, and RARP)
   B. IP Protocol (TCP, UDP, RIP, and OSPF)
   C. MAC address
   D. TCP or UDP port (HTTP = 80 and SMTP = 25)

6. Which of the following is generally not a function of the AP Web Server Setup page?
   A. Enable browsing to the web-based management system.
   B. Specify the location of the AP Help files.
   C. Enter settings for a custom-tailored web system for AP management.
   D. Filter out undesired websites over wireless access.

7.   Match the following AP radio pages to their proper functions.

1. AP Radio Port Link	A. Contains information about the operational status for the radio port of the AP. This page may also be used to make temporary changes in port status to help with troubleshooting network problems.
2. AP Radio Identification	B. Contains settings to configure protocol filters.
3. AP Radio Hardware	C. Contains SSID settings for the data rates, transmit power, antennas, radio channel, and operating thresholds of the AP.
4. AP Radio Filters	D. Lists key radio port configuration and statistical information for the AP.
5. AP Radio Advanced	E. Contains the basic locating and identity information for the AP radio port.

8.   Which of the following connection options are available on Cisco access points?
        A.   Console port
        B.   Telnet
        C.   Web browser.
        D.   All of the above

9.   Which of the following can be entered at the system prompt to display a list of commands available for each command mode?
        A.   help
        B.   ?
        C.   help?
        D.   list?
        E.   commands?

10.   Match the following error messages to their meaning.

1. % Ambiguous command: "show con"	A. The command is entered incorrectly. The caret ('^') marks the point of the error.
2. % Incomplete command.	B. Not enough characters entered for the access point to recognize the command.
3. % Invalid input detected at '^' marker.	C. Not all the keywords or parameters required by this command were entered.

11.   Which of the following can be entered at the system prompt to recall commands from the history buffer?

A. Press Ctrl-P or the up arrow key.
B. Press Ctrl-N or the down arrow key.
C. **show history**
D. All of the above

12. How often does the ACM read the client adapter status and update the status icon?
A. Thirty seconds
B. Two seconds
C. One minute
D. Five seconds

13. Match the access point modes to their descriptions.

1. Access Point Root (Fallback to Radio Island)	A. When the wired connection is lost, the radio becomes a repeater. The repeater parent should be configured to allow data to be wirelessly transferred to another access point.
2. Access Point Root (Fallback to Radio Shutdown)	B. This default setting enables wireless clients to continue to associate even when there is no connection to the wired LAN.
3. Access Point Root (Fallback to Repeater)	C. When the wired connection is lost, the radio shuts down. This fallback forces the clients to associate to another access point if one is available.
4. Repeater Non-Root	D. Choose this setting if the access point is not connected to the wired LAN. Client data is transferred to the access point selected as the repeater parent. The repeater parent may be configured as an access point or another repeater.

Notes

Chapter 6

Bridges

A *wireless bridge* is a link between one portion of a wireless local-area network (WLAN) and another. Bridges fill several rolls, depending on configuration. These options correspond to the following six roles, which a bridge can assume in a LAN:

- Root bridge
- Nonroot bridge with clients
- Nonroot bridge without clients
- Root access point (AP)
- Repeater AP
- Site survey client

The difference between these modes is whether or not the bridge is operating in root or nonroot mode—that is, as a parent or as a child. (A parent can share path information with its children.)

Bridge configuration is similar to AP configuration. It consists of assigning an IP address, subnet mask, and default gateway to the bridge.

With bridges comes the issue of path loss. This requires calculating the amount of power available in a link and subtracting various obstacles, including attenuation due to distance. If necessary, a gain antenna can be included in the link to help maintain an appropriate fade margin—that is, the amount of overhead in the path to keep it going in inclement conditions. External antennas also require protection against lighting. This ranges from installing lighting arrestors to installing short lengths of fiber-optic cable in the path to avoid forming a route to ground for lightning through your equipment.

Concept Questions

1. How many defined roles do bridges have? What are they?

_____
_____
_____
_____
_____
_____

2. Why is lightning a threat to network facilities that use wireless technology?

_____
_____

_____
_____
_____

3.   What are the considerations when deploying antennas for a wireless bridge?

_____
_____
_____
_____
_____

4.   Explain any significant differences in the radio module between Cisco Aironet wireless APs and wireless bridges.

_____
_____
_____
_____
_____

5.   What are some things to keep in mind when setting up antennas for wireless bridges?

_____
_____
_____
_____
_____

Vocabulary Exercise

authentication type

_____
_____
_____

bridge

_____
_____
_____
_____

Cisco Discovery Protocol (CDP)

_____
_____

coax

delay spread

fade margin

fiber-optic cabling

firmware

lightning arrestor

linear polarization

NEMA enclosure

_____

_____

_____

_____

nonroot bridge with clients

_____

_____

_____

_____

nonroot bridge without clients

_____

_____

_____

_____

nonroot mode

_____

_____

_____

_____

omnidirectional antennas

_____

_____

_____

_____

path loss

_____

_____

_____

_____

repeater AP

_____

_____

_____

_____

root AP

_____

_____

_____
_____

root bridge

_____
_____
_____
_____

root bridge mode

_____
_____
_____
_____

site survey client mode

_____
_____
_____
_____

Focus Questions

1.   What is a simple definition of a bridge?

_____
_____
_____
_____

2.   What is the role of a root bridge?

_____
_____
_____
_____

3.   At what OSI layer do bridges operate? What are the ramifications of this?

_____
_____
_____
_____

4.   In a given WLAN, how many bridges can function as the root bridge?

_____
_____

5.   Are Cisco Aironet bridges by default set as root bridges or nonroot bridges?

_____

_____

6.   What is the role of a nonroot bridge with clients?

_____

_____

_____

_____

7.   What is a repeater bridge?

_____

_____

_____

_____

8.   What is required for wireless clients to attach to a nonroot bridge?

_____

_____

_____

9.   What is the role of a nonroot bridge without clients?

_____

_____

_____

10.   What is the role of a root AP?

_____

_____

_____

_____

11.   What is the role of a repeater AP?

_____

_____

_____

_____

12.   What is the role of a site survey client?

_____

_____

_____

13. What are the two major categories for a bridge?

_____

_____

14. Unlike Cisco APs, bridges require some configuration prior to installation. What would this be?

_____

_____

_____

_____

15. What is the difference between a parent bridge and a child bridge?

_____

_____

_____

_____

16. What is one trick that you can use to extend the range of a WLAN?

_____

_____

_____

_____

17. What are some other ways to increase WLAN performance?

_____

_____

_____

_____

18. What kind of cabling does Cisco recommend as a means to protect the network from lightning?

_____

_____

19. Must a lightning bolt directly hit wireless equipment to cause productivity problems?

_____

_____

_____

20. Why should coax connectors be sealed?

_____

_____

_____

_____

21.　What is the allowable fade margin for WLAN radio frequency hops?

_____

_____

22.　What Cisco utility can help with path loss calculations?

_____

_____

23.　List four markets where WLAN bridging can be applied.

_____

_____

_____

_____

24.　What are some of the connection methods that can be used when configuring a bridge? (List three.)

_____

_____

_____

_____

25.　How many Ethernet-enabled devices does the WGB350 workgroup bridge support?

_____

_____

Review Questions

1.　Which of the following precautions will help ensure good link performance? (Select the best four answers.)
   A.　Minimize the distance between the bridge and the antenna to reduce signal loss.
   B.　Install the bridge away from microwave ovens or other devices that operate in the 2.4-GHz frequency range.
   C.　Review all cautions and warnings in the installation materials.
   D.　Secure the coax to the antenna mast with white nylon wire ties.
   E.　Situate the antennas for direct line-of-sight operation.

2.　What issues should you balance when planning a wireless bridge implementation? (Choose all that apply.)
   A.　Cost
   B.　Reliability
   C.　Risk of exposing birds to microwaves
   D.　Human health risk of microwaves
   E.　Distance
   F.　Data rate

3. Which item in a wireless bridge does not require periodic reading and updating?
   A. System firmware
   B. Radio firmware
   C. Web pages
   D. MAC address

4. Which of the following items must be on hand to properly install a wireless bridge configuration? (Choose all that apply.)
   A. The service set identifier (SSID) that will be used to identify the WLAN
   B. A system name for the bridge that describes the location or principal users of the bridge
   C. An IP address for the bridge if the network does not use DHCP to assign IP addresses
   D. A default gateway and an IP subnet mask for the bridge if the network uses subnets
   E. The MAC address for the bridge, which is printed on the label on the bottom of the bridge and which uniquely identifies the bridge on the WLAN

5. Identify methods of configuring a bridge. (Choose the best three.)
   A. The Web browser interface
   B. The USB memory device
   C. The command-line interface (CLI), using a terminal emulator or a Telnet session
   D. Replacement of the Flash card
   E. A Simple Network Management Protocol (SNMP) application

6. Match the following bridge roles to their proper descriptions.

1. Root Bridge	A. Use this setting for non-root bridges that accept associations with client devices, and for bridges acting as repeaters. Non-root bridges can communicate with other non-root bridges, root bridges, and client devices. A repeater bridge can be attached to a LAN segment, but does not need to be. Bridges set to non-root do not receive dynamic WEP keys for their data transmissions. Non-root bridges use the static WEP keys configured in their management systems.
2. Non-Root Bridge w/Clients	B. Use this setting when performing a site survey for a repeater access point. When you select this setting, clients are not allowed to associate and the bridge's STP function is disabled.

3. Non-Root Bridge w/o Clients	C. Use this setting to set up the bridge as a rugged access point connected to the wired LAN. When you select Access Point, the bridge's Spanning Tree Protocol (STP) function is disabled.
4. Root Access Point	D. Use this setting to set up the bridge as a rugged repeater access point. A repeater access point is not connected to the wired LAN; it is placed within radio range of an access point connected to the wired LAN to extend the range of your infrastructure or to overcome an obstacle that blocks radio communication. When you select Repeater, the bridge's STP function is disabled.
5. Repeater Access Point	E. Use this setting for non-root bridges that should not accept associations from client devices. A bridge set to Non-Root Bridge w/o Clients communicates only with another root or non-root bridge.
6. Site Survey Client	F. One bridge in each group of bridges must be set as the root bridge. A root bridge can only communicate with non-root bridges and other client devices and cannot associate with another root bridge. Use the Bridge Spacing setting to enter the distance between the root bridge and the non-root bridges with which it communicates.

7. What do the LEDs on the Cisco Aironet 1400 Series Wireless Bridge indicate?
   A. Install, Radio, Status
   B. Power, Radio, Status, and Ethernet
   C. Install, Radio, Status, and Ethernet
   D. Install, Power, Status, and Ethernet

8. Which of the following features in Cisco IOS Release 12.2(11)JA are supported by the 1400 series bridge?
   A. Broadcast key rotation
   B. Hot standby
   C. Multiple service set identifiers (SSIDs)
   D. Proxy Mobile IP
   E. World mode
   F. None of the above

Notes

Chapter 7

Antennas

To understand wireless networks, as well as how to set them up and optimize them for best performance, you need knowledge of antennas.

An antenna radiates transmitted signals or to capture received signals.

Antennas are of two main types: directional and omnidirectional.

Directional antennas radiate RF energy predominantly in one direction. The following are some common types of directional antennas:
- Yagi
- Solid parabolic
- Semiparabolic
- Patch or Panel

Omnidirectional antennas radiate RF energy equally in all horizontal directions. This horizontal radiation covers 360 degrees. Following are two common types of omnidirectional antennas:
- Mast mount
- Rubber dipole

Cisco antennas and all Cisco cables use a reverse polarity threaded naval connectors (RP-TNC). This connector looks like a TNC, but the center contacts have been reversed. This prohibits a standard off-the-shelf antenna from being attached to a Cisco radio frequency (RF) product.

Concept Questions

1. Why is the coverage area below an omnidirectional antenna poor?

_____
_____
_____
_____
_____

2. Why is the coverage area behind a directional antenna so poor?

_____
_____
_____
_____
_____

98

3.   Why is it important to keep antenna cable lengths short?

_____
_____
_____
_____
_____

4.   What is the main difference between planning a wired network and a wireless network?

_____
_____
_____
_____
_____

5.   What is the best way to mount an antenna to utilize its propagation characteristics?

_____
_____
_____
_____
_____

Vocabulary Exercise

absorption

_____
_____
_____

antenna array

_____
_____
_____

antenna diversity

_____
_____
_____

antenna electrical downtilt

_____
_____

bandwidth

beam

beamwidth

dipole antenna

directional antenna

diversity

Effective Isotropic Radiated Power (EIRP)

fading

_____

_____

_____

_____

Fresnel zone

_____

_____

_____

_____

frequency diversity

_____

_____

_____

_____

gain

_____

_____

_____

_____

ground plane

_____

_____

_____

_____

harmonic

_____

_____

_____

_____

impedence

_____

_____

_____

_____

isotropic antenna

_____

_____

lightning arrestor

margin

overall link quality

patch antenna

path analysis

polarization

power

receiver

_____

_____

splitters

_____

_____

_____

_____

transmitter

_____

_____

_____

_____

Focus Questions

1. What are the two main types of antenna?

_____

_____

2. Why is impedance match important for antenna cabling and connectors?

_____

_____

3. Why does the U.S Federal Communications Commission (FCC) require each wireless LAN vendor to use different connectors for their antennas?

_____

_____

4. What is the best way to know the functional distance between wireless LAN equipment?

_____

5. What measurement unit does gain use to express respect to an isotropic antenna?

_____

6. What measurement unit is used to express antenna gain with respect to a dipole antenna?

_____

7. What measurement unit is used to express antenna gain with respect to the milliwatt?

_____

8.   In an RF link, what happens if both antennas do not have the same polarization?

_____

9.   What is a theoretical antenna having coverage in all directions referred to as?

_____

10.   What antenna setting is used as a means of achieving an improvement in the system reliability for the problem of multipath fading?

_____

11.   What are the two different types of diversity?

_____

12.   What is the solution to overcoming the poor coverage area of an omnidirectional antenna?

_____

13.   Is a long-range omnidirectional antenna horizontally or vertically polarized?

_____

14.   Is a Yagi antenna omnidirectional or directional?

_____

15.   Why must wireless local-area network (WLAN) administrators be concerned with long antenna cable lengths?

_____
_____
_____

16.   Why must outdoor coaxial cable connections be sealed?

_____
_____

17.   What are the two main purposes of a lightning arrestor in the antenna installation process?

_____
_____

18.   What is the Fresnel zone?

_____
_____

19.   At what distance does the Earth's bulge become a concern for the installation of the RF antenna link?

_____

20.   How is the Earth's bulge obstruction overcome in an RF antenna installation?

_____
_____

Review Questions

1.   What are the two types of antennas referenced for wireless LAN applications?
    A.   Static and dynamic
    B.   Omnidirectional and directional
    C.   Aluminum and copper
    D.   Radio and television

2.   What type of wireless RF antenna and cable connector does Cisco Aironet use?
    A.   RP-TNC connector
    B.   AUI connector
    C.   British Navy connector
    D.   RJ-45 connector

3.   How is antenna gain referenced to a dipole antenna represented?
    A.   dBi
    B.   dBm
    C.   dBd
    D.   dB

4.   What are the two types of antenna polarization?
    A.   Length and width
    B.   Horizontal and vertical
    C.   Indoor and outdoor
    D.   Left and right

5.   What solves the problem of multipath fading for WLAN antenna RF signals?
    A.   The data rate setting
    B.   The channel setting
    C.   The wired equivalent privacy (WEP) setting
    D.   The antenna diversity setting

Notes

Chapter 8

Security

What is network security? *Network security* is the process by which digital information assets are protected. The goals of security are to maintain integrity, protect confidentiality, and ensure availability. Why have security? The growth of computing has generated enormous advances in the way people live and work. With this in mind, it is imperative that all networks be protected from threats and vulnerabilities so that the Internet can achieve its fullest potential.

It is impossible to eliminate or prevent security risks completely. Effective risk management and assessments can significantly minimize the existing security risks to an acceptable level. The level of acceptability depends on how much risk the individual or stakeholders are willing to assume. Generally, the risk is worth assuming if the cost of implementing the risk-reducing safeguards far exceeds the benefits.

The three goals of security are integrity, confidentiality, and availability.

Wireless local-area network (WLAN) devices have security weaknesses that must be recognized and protected against. These weaknesses include password protection and lack of authentication.

Concept Questions

1. What are the goals of network security?

2. What security precautions were used in the first generation of WLANs?

3. What are the three main sections that are configured on the access point (AP) to secure the WLAN?

4.   What is accomplished by enabling protocol filtering and MAC filtering on the wireless AP?

5.   What is the advantage of using Cisco Lightweight EAP (LEAP) in your Cisco WLAN?

Vocabulary Exercise

AAA

access attack

ACS

active scanning

AES

_____
_____
_____
_____

association

_____
_____
_____
_____

authentication

_____
_____
_____
_____

authentication, authorization, and accounting (AAA)

_____
_____
_____
_____

authentication phase

_____
_____
_____
_____

availability

_____
_____
_____
_____

CHAP

_____
_____
_____
_____

Cisco Lightweight EAP (LEAP) authentication type

_____
_____

110

client impersonation

confidentiality

denial of service (DoS)

DES

dictionary attacks

dynamic key derivation

EAP

EAPOL

_____
_____
_____
_____

encryption

_____
_____
_____
_____

external threats

_____
_____
_____
_____

GSS_API (Kerberos)

_____
_____
_____
_____

integrity

_____
_____
_____
_____

Internet Key Exchange (IKE)

_____
_____
_____
_____

LDAP

_____
_____
_____
_____

LEAP

_____
_____

MAC address filtering

MIC

mutual authentication

network security

open authentication

open authentication scheme

OTP

113

passive monitoring

_____
_____
_____
_____

Probe phase

_____
_____
_____
_____

protocol filtering

_____
_____
_____
_____

RADIUS

_____
_____
_____
_____

RC4 encryption algorithm

_____
_____
_____
_____

reconnaissance attack

_____
_____
_____
_____

rogue AP

_____
_____
_____
_____

service set identifier (SSID)

_____
_____

114

shared key authentication

structured threats

threats

transport layer

Transport Layer Security (TLS)

unstructured threats

VPN

wired equivalent privacy (WEP)

_____

_____

_____

_____

Focus Questions

1. What are the three primary network security weaknesses? Define them.

    _____

    _____

    _____

2. What are the four primary network security threats? Define them.

    _____

    _____

    _____

    _____

3. What are the three primary attack methods on a network?

    _____

    _____

    _____

4. What are the four steps to securing your network?

    _____

    _____

    _____

    _____

5. What is the first step in security design?

    _____

    _____

    _____

6. The IEEE 802.11b standard attempts to provide "privacy of a wire" via an optional encryption scheme called what?

    _____

    _____

7. What parts comprise a WEP key?

    _____

    _____

    _____

8.   What are the three states of the authentication and association process of an AP and client?

_____

_____

_____

9.   What are the two types of authentication methods defined by IEEE 802.11?

_____

_____

10.   How do you protect your wireless AP from unauthorized users from changing its configuration?

_____

_____

11.   What are the four steps for enabling WEP on the AP?

_____

_____

_____

_____

12.   What three methods can you use to filter data on your wireless network?

_____

_____

_____

13.   What are three disposition settings on the protocol filter setting?

_____

_____

_____

14.   Why would a network administrator set up MAC address filtering on the AP?

_____

_____

_____

_____

15.   What is the purpose of the Association Table Display Setup?

_____

_____

_____

_____

16.   What are the components of the AAA environment?

_____

_____

Review Questions

1.   True or False: The SSID is transmitted in clear text form and is not a security feature.

2.   Which of the following methods is considered a passive attack?
A.   Access attack
B.   Denial of service (DoS) attack
C.   Reconnaissance attack
D.   Shaq attack

3.   Which is the more secure authentication method for an AP?
A.   Shared key authentication
B.   Open authentication

4.   Which of the following terms refers to leaving the SSID parameter blank on a wireless client and will associate to any AP regardless of SSID setting on AP?
A.   "Null" string
B.   "No" string
C.   "SSID NULL"
D.   "SSID NONE"

5.   What encryption algorithm does WEP use?
A.   The RC4 algorithm
B.   The RC2 algorithm
C.   The RC6 algorithm
D.   The RC8 algorithm

6.   What is the length of the Initialization Vector (IV) used in WEP?
A.   24 bits
B.   40 bits
C.   64 bits
D.   128 bits

7.   What is the process of verifying the credentials of a client who wants to join a WLAN?
A.   Association
B.   Authentication
C.   Verification
D.   Network control

8.   Which encryption parameter requires client devices to use WEP when communicating with the AP?
    A.   No Encryption (default)
    B.   Full Encryption
    C.   Optional
    D.   Open encrption

9.   Which IEEE standard addresses 802.11 security issues?
    A.   802.1g
    B.   802.1x
    C.   802.1a
    D.   802.1b

10.   Which database can the RADIUS server check for user authentication?
    A.   Windows server
    B.   Oracle administration
    C.   Apple User database
    D.   NetWare database

11.   What port parameter setting is used for the Cisco RADIUS server on the AP?
    A.   Port 1812
    B.   Port 1645
    C.   Port 81
    D.   Port 23

Notes

Chapter 9

Application Design and Site Survey Preparation

Why is a site survey important? Before you install wireless local-area network (WLAN) access points (APs), you should investigate a few things about the customer's facility. A good site survey helps determine the following:

- Feasibility of the desired coverage
- Radio frequency interference (RFI)Wired connectivity limitations

A site survey allows the customer to properly install the WLAN and have consistent, reliable wireless access. A WLAN site survey engineer should be knowledgeable about both wireless and wired equipment.

A site survey helps the customer determine how many APs are necessary throughout the facility to provide the desired coverage. The survey also determines the placement of those APs and details the necessary information for installation.

In addition, a site survey determines the feasibility of the desired coverage in the face of obstacles such as wired connectivity limitations, radio hazards, and application requirements. This allows the customer to properly install the WLAN and have consistent, reliable wireless access.

The process of performing a site survey includes the following steps:

Step 1. Gather the tools and the configuration.

Step 2. Research and investigate industry-specific concerns.

Step 3. Gather the recommended equipment list (site survey kit).

Step 4. Implement the site survey.

Step 5. Document the site survey.

Concept Questions

1.   Operating conditions are conditions that are directly involved in the operation of your WLAN network or equipment. Environmental conditions are those conditions in the environmental area within your (affecting) WLAN network. What are some operating and environmental conditions that need to be considered in the site survey?

_____

_____

_____
_____
_____
_____
_____
_____
_____

2. What productivity benefits can you achieve if you implement a wireless
    LAN in the job industry where you are employed?

_____
_____
_____
_____
_____
_____
_____
_____

3. The four main design requirements for a WLAN solution are availability,
    scalability, manageability, and interoperability. Explain how to achieve
    each of them.

_____
_____
_____
_____
_____
_____
_____
_____
_____

4. The main factor to take into account when designing building-to-building
    WLANs is path considerations between the radio's line of sight. List and
    explain the path considerations.

_____
_____
_____

5. Why is it so important for the WLAN site survey engineer to have a properly
stocked site survey kit?

_____
_____
_____
_____

Vocabulary Exercise

attenuator

_____
_____
_____
_____

auto rate negotiation

_____
_____
_____
_____

availability

_____
_____
_____
_____

BSA

_____
_____
_____
_____

collision avoidance (CSMA/CA)

_____
_____
_____
_____

Constantly Awake Mode

_____
_____
_____
_____

dedicated pipe

_____
_____
_____
_____

electromagnetic field probe

_____

_____

_____

_____

encryption

_____

_____

_____

fade margin

_____

_____

_____

_____

Fast Power Save Mode (FastPSP)

_____

_____

_____

_____

frequency counter

_____

_____

_____

_____

interference

_____

_____

_____

_____

interoperability

_____

_____

_____

_____

line of sight (LOS)

_____

_____

management

micro cell

mobile users

obstructions

"pools" of coverage

Power Save Mode (PSP)

rate shift

reverse polarity threaded naval connectors (RP-TNC)

_____

_____

_____

_____

scalability

_____

_____

_____

_____

shared pipe

_____

_____

_____

_____

site survey

_____

_____

_____

_____

site walkthrough

_____

_____

_____

_____

spectrum analyzer

_____

_____

_____

_____

system redundancy

_____

_____

_____

_____

topology of WLANs

_____

_____

Focus Questions

1. Why is a site survey important?

2. Why must a clear LOS be maintained between wireless bridge antennas?

3. What is the basic service area, also referred to as a BSS?

4. What agency governs the use of wireless devices on airplanes?

5. What device is used for wireless clients to communicate together within a small office, home office (SOHO) topology?

6. What is a benefit of using WLAN devices in a retail setting?

7. Why are Healthcare site surveys some of the most restricting, time-consuming, and difficult site surveys?

8. For what applications are WLAN devices used in the hotel industry?

9. Why is performing a site survey at an airport considered much easier than at a hospital?

10. What are some of the factors that limit the link speed of a radio frequency (RF) connection?

_____

_____

_____

_____

_____

11. At what speed do many data collection WLAN devices operate?

_____

_____

12. What are the maximum possible WLAN APs that are co-located in one area when using 802.11b technology?

_____

_____

13. If you are using multiple APs and you want to achieve a total aggregate of 11 Mbps, what setting will the APs be configured to?

_____

_____

14. What power save mode should be used on wireless clients when power is not an issue?

_____

_____

15. What is one method that can be used so that interference can be avoided in your WLAN?

_____

_____

16. What are three encryption options that are available for WLANs?

_____

_____

17. What IEEE standard is enhancing the use of security in wireless networks?

_____

_____

18. What are some of the challenges involved in building-to-building wireless networking design?

_____

_____

_____

19.   How is the Fresnel zone important in a building-to-building wireless networking design?

_____

_____

Review Questions

1.   True or False: A site survey is completed only after the installation of the WLAN.

2.   Which industry site is considered the most difficult to survey?
   A.   Airports
   B.   Retail stores
   C.   Hospitals
   D.   Warehouses

3.   Which of the four design requirements is concerned with system redundancy?
   A.   Availability
   B.   Scalability
   C.   Manageability
   D.   Interoperability

4.   What is the proper antenna configuration to use in a point-to-multipoint configuration, where the links are greater than a mile?
   A.   Use an omnidirectional dipole antenna at the main site and use omnidirectional dipole antennas at the remote sites.
   B.   Use a high-gain omnidirectional antenna at the main site and use high-gain directional antennas at the remotes sites.
   C.   Use a high-gain directional antenna at the main site and use high-gain directional antennas at each remote site.
   D.   Use a low-gain directional antenna at the main site and use low-gain directional antennas at each remote site.

5.   What can you use instead of carrying one of every length of cable, lightning arrestors, splitters, and other accessories?
   A.   Outfit the site survey kit with an antenna attenuator.
   B.   Outfit the site survey kit with an antenna patch cord.
   C.   Outfit the site survey kit with an antenna connector.
   D.   Outfit the site survey kit with an antenna sealant.

Notes

Chapter 10

Site Survey

By providing the customer with a detailed site survey report, an IT manager can turn the necessary portions over to a local contractor who can install any cabling needed to provide wireless local-area network (WLAN) devices connectivity to the network.

Installers need a site survey that provides detailed information about where the APs are to be located, how they will be mounted, how they will be connected to the network, and where any cabling or power may need to be installed.

At the same time, you can make preparations on the customer's network for the upcoming installation.

Try to identify potential problems up front and discuss how these issues will be handled.

This discovery can potentially save much time and trouble during the installation. By addressing potential problems and being proactive instead of reactive, the site survey engineer is viewed as the strong, reliable source during installation, instead of the weak link.

Concept Questions

1. Why is it important to examine a customer's existing network prior to performing a site survey?

_____
_____
_____
_____
_____

2. What is an easy way to start a site survey?

_____
_____
_____
_____
_____
_____
_____

3.   Why is it important to decide where and how the access points (APs) will be mounted?

_____

_____

_____

_____

_____

4.   What must the network administrator be aware of when installing cable extensions and connectors into a WLAN?

_____

_____

_____

5.   Why is it necessary to go through the additional work of responding to a customer request for proposal (RFP) with a design document?

_____

_____

_____

_____

_____

_____

_____

_____

6.   What are some of the customer's responsibilities in the project management of a WLAN implementation?

_____

_____

_____

_____

_____

Vocabulary Exercise

baseline of network performance

_____

_____

_____

building risers

_____

_____

_____

_____

bulkhead extender

_____
_____
_____
_____

Category 5 (Cat 5) unshielded twisted-pair (UTP)

_____
_____
_____
_____

Cisco Network Designer (CND)

_____
_____
_____
_____

ConfigMaker

_____
_____
_____
_____

content-addressable memory (CAM)

_____
_____
_____
_____

dead spot

_____
_____
_____
_____

design document

_____
_____
_____
_____

electromagnetic interference (EMI)

_____
_____

fudge factor

lightning arrestor

LOS

MAC CRC errors

NEMA enclosures

network health checklist

network map

nonoverlapping channels

_____
_____
_____
_____

plenum

_____
_____
_____
_____

plenum cables

_____
_____
_____
_____

request for proposal (RFP)

_____
_____
_____
_____

service loops

_____
_____
_____
_____

virtual private networks (VPNs)

_____
_____
_____
_____

Focus Questions

1.   What is a presite survey?

_____
_____
_____
_____
_____

2.   Why should you examine a customer's existing network prior to conducting a site survey for WLAN implementation?

_____

_____

3.   What happens if the customer cannot provide a detailed and up-to-date map of the existing network?

_____

_____

_____

4.   What is the maximum distance that you can run a length of Cat 5 UTP for a data link?

_____

_____

5.   What is a building riser?

_____

_____

6.   Why should you study the performance of the existing network?

_____

_____

_____

_____

7.   Why should you perform a site-to-site survey with a radio frequency (RF) spectrum analyzer?

_____

_____

_____

_____

_____

8.   What can occur with your RF signal of the access point if you place it in a corner of an area near the outer walls?

_____

_____

9.   At what data rate should you perform your survey?

_____

_____

10. Will you always be able to perform a site survey and design 100 percent coverage of the area?

_____

_____

11. What is a possible solution when the environment is too harsh to install an AP in it, even with a NEMA enclosure?

_____

_____

_____

12. What special caution needs to be taken when surveying multifloor facilities?

_____

_____

13. Why is it a good idea to seal antenna connections?

_____

_____

14. What should you consider before using an antenna with a 100-foot extension cable?

_____

_____

15. What connector type is used on the Cisco Aironet products?

_____

_____

16. How much loss will a splitter add to your WLAN antenna system?

_____

_____

17. Can you easily add an amplifier to your WLAN system if you want to extend its range?

_____

_____

_____

18. How can you protect your wired network from a direct lightning strike to the wireless network antenna?

_____

_____

Review Questions

1. What device can you use to check the site survey area for interference?
   A. AM-FM radio
   B. RF spectrum analyzer
   C. Microwave oven
   D. Cisco Network Design (CND) application software

2. For a standard survey, how much overlap is usually sufficient to provide for smooth, transparent handoffs?
   A. 10%
   B. 15%
   C. 20%
   D. 25%

3. How many nonoverlapping channels are used in 802.11b WLANs?
   A. 2
   B. 3
   C. 4
   D. 5

4. True or False: Water is good for antenna connections and amplifies the RF signal better.

5. Which of the following WLAN devices add gain to the WLAN antenna system?
   A. Antenna
   B. Antenna connectors
   C. Extension cables
   D. Attenuators
   E. Splitters

Notes

Chapter 11

Troubleshooting Management, Monitoring, and Diagnostics

Complex network environments mean that the potential for connectivity and performance problems in a network is high, and the source of problems is often elusive.

The keys to maintaining a problem-free network environment, as well as maintaining the ability to isolate and fix a network fault quickly, are documentation, planning, and communication.

This requires a framework of procedures and personnel to be in place long before network changes take place. The goal of this chapter is to help you isolate and resolve the most common connectivity and performance problems in your network environment.

Troubleshooting networks, including WLANs, is more important than ever. Networks continue to add services as time goes on, and with each added service comes more variables involved in implementing networks.

This adds to the complexity of troubleshooting the networks. Therefore, organizations increasingly depend on network administrators and network engineers having strong troubleshooting skills.

Troubleshooting is arguably the process that takes the greatest percentage of a network engineer's time. That is why any procedural tools that can be used to simplify the process are welcome.

Of course, with each procedural tool comes the time required to internalize it, so decisions come down to how much time must be spent "up front" versus "in the field." These types of decisions are not easy to make; finding the right balance comes with experience.

One of the main goals is to optimize your time up front to help shorten your time in the field.

Concept Questions

1. Why is troubleshooting considered "an exercise in logic"?

_____

_____

2.   Why is it important for a network administrator to understand the OSI model when troubleshooting a network?

_____

_____

_____

_____

_____

3.   Why should the network administrator be concerned about TCP/IP if he is using a wireless network that employs RF signals for connections?

_____

_____

_____

_____

_____

4.   Why should the network administrator be proficient with network monitoring hardware tools as well as available software applications?

_____

_____

_____

_____

_____

_____

5.   How important is it to understand specific problems and single point failures in troubleshooting a wireless network?

_____

_____

_____

_____

6.   By now, you've probably noticed that some of the most common network problems can be attributed to cable issues, including media, connectors, and patch panels. What is a good method for troubleshooting a cable connection?

_____

_____

_____

_____

7.   Why is it important to monitor your network even when it is operating efficiently?

_____

_____

_____

_____

_____

Vocabulary Exercise

accounting management

_____

_____

_____

_____

AP mismatches

_____

_____

_____

_____

bridging loops

_____

_____

_____

_____

communication range

_____

_____

_____

_____

configuration management

_____

_____

_____

_____

deductive reasoning

_____

_____

_____

_____

144

event logs

_____
_____
_____
_____

fault management

_____
_____
_____
_____

fault management steps

_____
_____
_____
_____
_____

FDDI

_____
_____
_____
_____

field strength

_____
_____
_____
_____

firmware version

_____
_____
_____
_____

hypotheses

_____
_____
_____

inductive reasoning

_____
_____

Internet Control Message Protocol (ICMP)

Internet protocols

ipconfig

ISO Network Management Model

nbstat

netstat

network analyzer

nslookup

_____

_____

_____

_____

optical time domain reflectometer (OTDR)

_____

_____

_____

_____

OSI reference model

_____

_____

_____

_____

performance management

_____

_____

_____

_____

ping

_____

_____

_____

_____

reflectometer

_____

_____

_____

_____

scientific method

_____

_____

_____

_____

_____

security management

_____
_____
_____
_____

Simple Network Management Protocol (SNMP)

_____
_____
_____
_____

sniffer

_____
_____
_____
_____

spectrum analyzer

_____
_____
_____
_____

systematic approach

_____
_____
_____
_____

TDR

_____
_____
_____
_____

Telnet

_____
_____
_____
_____

tracert

_____
_____

Focus Questions

1. What are the keys to maintaining a problem-free network environment?

    _____
    _____
    _____

2. How can you properly analyze a network problem?

    _____
    _____

3. What is network troubleshooting?

    _____
    _____

4. What can be the most important requirement in any network environment?

    _____
    _____
    _____

5. What is network management?

    _____
    _____
    _____
    _____
    _____

6. What are the steps involved in network troubleshooting?

    _____
    _____
    _____
    _____
    _____

7. What does the OSI reference model describe?

    _____
    _____
    _____

8.   List some Layer 1 problems in a network.

_____

_____

_____

_____

9.   At what layer does wireless bridging occur?

_____

_____

_____

10.   What is a bridging loop?

_____

_____

_____

11.   List some common TCP/IP troubleshooting commands.

_____

_____

12.   List some of the third-party tools that are available to troubleshoot networks.

_____

_____

_____

_____

_____

13.   What is a (network) packet sniffer?

_____

_____

_____

_____

14.   What task does a spectrum analyzer perform?

_____

_____

_____

_____

15.   Why is it advisable to use the most recent version of a driver or firmware with your WLAN products?

_____

_____

16. Why must WLAN devices be set to the same service set identifier (SSID)?

_____

_____

17. Why is it important that WLAN device settings for frequencies be set as automatic?

_____

_____

_____

18. What problems might you encounter with cables that connect to WLAN devices?

_____

_____

_____

19. Can anyone install a high-gain antenna onto his wireless LAN that exceeds 36 dBm if it is installed on the 802.11b 2.4 GHz unregulated frequency?

_____

_____

_____

_____

20. What are some typical problems that can go wrong with the Category 5 UTP LAN cable in a network?

_____

_____

21. What device is designed to lessen congestion to your network, hubs, or switches?

_____

_____

_____

22. What is one of the best methods to monitor your WLAN access points (APs) and bridges?

_____

_____

_____

Review Questions

1. What process takes the greatest percentage of a network engineer's time?
    A. Turning on the computers
    B. Troubleshooting the network
    C. Backing up data
    D. Adding new software applications

2. Which of the following are considered Layer 2 problems? (Choose all that apply.)
    A. Improperly configured Ethernet interfaces
    B. Broken cables
    C. Improperly configured serial interfaces
    D. Cables that are connected to the wrong ports
    E. Improper clock rate settings on serial interfaces

3. Which of the following commands is most appropriately used to find the IP address of a host?
    A. **ping**
    B. **tracert**
    C. **ipconfig**
    D. **telnet**

4. Which of the following are used to troubleshoot a network problem? (Choose all that apply.)
    A. Volt-ohmmeters
    B. Digital multimeters
    C. OTDR
    D. Cable testers

5. True or False: In many instances, line of sight is not seen to be a problem, particularly for WLAN devices that communicate over short distances.

6. An SNMP-managed network consists of three key components: What are they? (Choose all that apply.)
    A. Managed devices
    B. Agents
    C. Network management systems (NMSs)
    D. Cabling
    E. WAN services

7. Which of the following are valid functions that the **show** command can be used to perform?
    A. Isolate problem interfaces, nodes, media, or applications
    B. Monitor normal network operation
    C. Monitor router behavior during initial installation

D.   Determine the status of servers, clients, or other neighbors

E.   All of the above

8.   The _____ tool on a Windows NT, 2000, or XP host reports each node a TCP/IP packet crosses on its way to a destination. It essentially does the same thing as the **trace** command in the Cisco IOS Software.

A.   **ping**

B.   **traceroute**

C.   **tracert**

D.   **ip trace**

9.   Which item(s) can cause interference and signal degradation?

A.   Radio interference

B.   Electromagnetic interference

C.   Cordless phones or other 2.4-GHz wireless devices

D.   All of the above

Notes

Chapter 12

Emerging Technologies

Previous chapters covered current wireless standards and technologies, Cisco Aironet wireless products, and how to configure them. In this chapter, you learn about new and emerging wireless technologies, both fixed and mobile.

Concept Questions

1. What new wireless applications do you anticipate in the years to come?

   _____

   _____

   _____

   _____

   _____

2. What major benefits will be derived from wireless Voice over IP (VoIP) devices?

   _____

   _____

   _____

   _____

   _____

3. How are mobile wireless communications similar to WLAN networking?

   _____

   _____

   _____

   _____

   _____

   _____

   _____

4. Why is an organization such as the Wireless LAN Association (WLANA) necessary?

   _____

   _____

   _____

   _____

   _____

   _____

   _____

5. What benefits would a wireless local-area network (WLAN) implementation at your employment site reap?

_____
_____
_____
_____
_____

6. What are the major components of a VoIP network?

_____
_____
_____
_____

7. Name the types of messages that the H.323 standard uses to facilitate communication.

_____
_____
_____
_____
_____

Vocabulary Exercise

1G

_____
_____
_____
_____

3G

_____
_____
_____
_____

baseband

_____
_____
_____

Bipolar Modulation Scheme

_____
_____

Certified Wireless Network Professional (CWNP) Program

Cisco Wireless LAN Design Specialist (CWLDS)

Cisco Wireless LAN Support Specialist (CWLSS)

code division multiple access (CDMA)

code division multiple access 2000 (CDMA 2000)

coder-decoder (codec) compression schemes

Computing Technology Industry Association (CompTIA)

common channel signaling

_____

_____

_____

_____

digital signal processor

_____

_____

_____

_____

enhanced data rates for global evolution (EDGE)

_____

_____

_____

_____

ENUM (telephone number resolution)

_____

_____

_____

_____

European Telecommunications Standards Institute (ETSI)

_____

_____

_____

_____

Federal Communications Commission (FCC)

_____

_____

_____

_____

frequency division multiple access (FDMA)

_____

_____

_____

_____

frequency domain

_____

_____

159

general packet radio service (GPRS)

Global Positioning System (GPS)

global system for mobile communication (GSM)

H.323

handling delay

IEEE 802.11e

interference

jamming resistance

_____
_____
_____
_____

jitter

_____
_____
_____
_____

Media Gateway (MG)

_____
_____
_____
_____

Media Gateway Control Protocol (MGCP)

_____
_____
_____
_____

Media Gateway Controller (MGC)

_____
_____
_____
_____

mobile telephone switching office (MTSO)

_____
_____
_____
_____

Mobile Wireless Internet Forum (MWIF)

_____
_____
_____
_____

multipath interference

_____
_____

National Association of Communications Systems Engineers (NACSE)

network layer

network type

notch filters

Open Mobile Alliance (OMA)

PCM

PPP

quality of service (QoS)

_____
_____
_____
_____

Real Time Streaming Protocol (RTSP)

_____
_____
_____
_____

Real-Time Transport Protocol

_____
_____
_____
_____

Resource Reservation Protocol (RSVP)

_____
_____
_____
_____

RTP Control Protocol (RTCP)

_____
_____
_____
_____

Session Announcement Protocol

_____
_____
_____
_____

Session Description Protocol (SDP)

_____
_____
_____
_____

Session Initiation Protocol

_____
_____

session layer

_____
_____
_____
_____

Signaling System 7 (SS7)

_____
_____
_____
_____

softswitch

_____
_____
_____
_____

spatial capacity

_____
_____
_____
_____

time division multiplex access (TDMA)

_____
_____
_____
_____

time domain

_____
_____
_____
_____

ultra-wideband (UWB)

_____
_____
_____
_____

Underwriters Laboratories (UL)

_____

_____

_____

_____

Voice over IP (VoIP) or IP telephony

_____

_____

_____

_____

WAP Data Gram Protocol (WDP)

_____

_____

_____

_____

WAP Session Protocol (WSP)

_____

_____

_____

_____

WAP Transaction Protocol (WTP)

_____

_____

_____

_____

wideband code division multiple access (WCDMA)

_____

_____

_____

_____

Wi-Fi zone

_____

_____

_____

_____

Wireless Ethernet Compatibility Alliance (WECA)

_____

_____

Wireless Fidelity (WiFi) Alliance

_____
_____
_____
_____

Wireless LAN Association (WLANA)

_____
_____
_____
_____

Wireless Markup Language (WML)

_____
_____
_____
_____

wireless transport layer security (WTLS)

_____
_____
_____
_____

Review Questions

1. What agency sets the rules for radiated emissions of intentional radiators in the United States?
   A. WLANA
   B. WiFi
   C. FCC
   D. ETSI
   E. UL

2. What is QoS in networking?
   A. QoS means to provide data with the type of transport service that it needs.
   B. QoS means to ensure that data cables are of high grade.
   C. QoS means that customer service representatives are available to the customer at least 8 hours a day.
   D. QoS means that all personnel who are handling your network have achieved the appropriate certification level.

3.   What association was formed in 1999 to certify interoperability of WLAN products?
      A.   WLANA
      B.   WiFi
      C.   FCC
      D.   ETSI
      E.   UL

4.   What association or agency promotes the use of wireless networking technology and works to raise consumer awareness regarding the use and availability of WLANs?
      A.   WLANA
      B.   WiFi
      C.   FCC
      D.   ETSI
      E.   UL

5.   Which agency or organization is a not-for-profit organization whose mission is to produce the telecommunications standards to be used throughout Europe and beyond?
      A.   WLANA
      B.   WiFi
      C.   FCC
      D.   ETSI
      E.   UL

6.   What agency or organization is an independent, not-for-profit product safety testing and certification organization?
      A.   UL
      B.   WLAN
      C.   WiFi
      D.   FCC
      E.   ETSI

7.   Per U.S. FCC regulations, what can UWB devices be used for?
      A.   Precise measurement of distances or locations.
      B.   Obtaining the images of objects buried under ground or behind surfaces
      C.   Wireless communications, particularly for short-range, high-speed data transmissions
      D.   All of the above

8.   What are three benefits of Voice over IP? (Select three.)
      A.   Cost savings
      B.   Open standards
      C.   Integrated voice and data networks
      D.   Ease of integration
      E.   Ease of maintenance

Notes

Appendix A

Answers to the Review Questions

Chapter 1

1. *Thinnet*, *Thicknet*, and *Cheapernet* all refer to which pre-802.11 media that is still popular for the transmission of video?
    D. Coaxial cable

2. What is it called when signals from one pair of wires in a cable appear in a different pair?
    A. Cross talk

3. Which of the following is *not* an advantage of wireless technology?
    E. No need for wired infrastructure

4. Starting with the most intimate and ending with the most global, order the following types of network: personal-area network (PAN), local-area network (LAN), wide-area network (WAN), and metropolitan-area network (MAN).
    C. PAN, LAN, MAN, WAN

5. Which of the following groups use primarily wireless technology?
    F. All of the above

6. Which of the following devices may cause interference in a wireless network?
    D. A and C

7. Which of the following are used in Layer 1 of the OSI model?
    F. All of the above

Chapter 2

1. Which of the following is not an advantage of standardization?
    B. Quicker obsolescence

2. What is the role of IEEE in WLAN activities?
    C. Promote and update the 802.11 standard and its versions

3. Which of the following is the least accurate statement?
    F. A common distribution system can connect multiple BSS and IBSS, and it must be wireless.

4. Which of the following is the biggest disadvantage of 802.11a?
   A. It uses the 5-GHz frequency band, instead of 2.4 GHz, precluding backward compatibility.

5. Which of the following is not an advantage of the IR PHY standard?
   B. It has a range of only about 20 meters maximum.
   C. It will operate only in indoor environments.

Chapter 3

1. Which of the following is least likely to be an important use of radio in the home?
   H. Television remote control units

2. A dB has no particular defined reference and can refer to any change of power. In measurements where the same reference is used to compare many things, the reference value is usually written after the dB. What is the symbol for dB with reference to hypothetically perfect antenna?
   C. dB isotropic (dBi)

3. The electromagnetic (EM) spectrum is simply a name that scientists have given to the set of all types of radiation, when discussed as a group. Which of the following is *not* an example of radiation in the electromagnetic (EM) spectrum? (Choose two.)
   C. Music that comes from a CD player
   F. Wind

4. Which of the following is a valid frequency for Wi-Fi? Choose all that apply.
   B. 2.4–2.4835 GHz (US ISM Band)
   C. 5.725 GHz–5.850 GHz

5. Correctly order the following steps of the A to D process.
   1) Assign a discrete value to each sample.
   2) Sample analog wave amplitudes at specific instances in time.
   3) Convert each discrete value to a stream of bits.
   4) Transmit or store the stream of bits as required by the application.
   D. 2-1-3-4

6. What does the description "A disturbance or variation that transfers energy progressively from point to point in a medium" define?
   B. A wave

7. Correctly order the following types of electromagnetic waves in order of increasing frequency and energy, and decreasing wavelength.
   1) radio waves
   2) visible light

3) infrared light
4) microwaves
C.   1-4-3-2

Chapter 4

1. How does an increase in user mobility result in an increase in productivity? (Choose three.)
   B.   Users can be connected to corporate files and resources while they are in the meeting.
   C.   There is less personal preparation copying files; users can simply pick up and go, with all of their resources available.
   D.   Instant messaging, e-mail, printing, files, and Internet access are all easily accessible.

2. Which of the following is not a commonly available user interface for handheld computers?
   E.   Fully functional operating system

3. Which of the following is a consideration for choosing mobile devices for integration into your WLAN?
   D.   Presence of AC power near all APs

4. You should carefully choose antennas to provide optimum coverage for the installation without offering opportunities for interference or snooping. Which of the following is not an important distinction among antennas?
   B.   Type and length of mounting screws

5. Many corporations are supplying their workforce with laptops instead of desktop models. While workers are in the office, the laptop is typically connected to a docking station with a large display monitor, full-size keyboard, and a mouse for improved ergonomic use. Which of the following is not an advantage of this approach?
   D.   Laptop hard drives contain sensitive corporate data.

Chapter 5

1. Load balancing on an AP is set to automatically direct client devices to an AP that provides the best connection to the network. Which of the following features can be used to set load balancing? (Choose three.)
   A.   Number of users
   C.   Bit error rates
   D.   Signal strength

2.	Which of the following are not roles of wireless APs?
	B.	An AP can protect network users against electromagnetic interference (EMI) and radio frequency interface (RFI).

3.	Before you set up an AP, what information should you gather? (Select the best six answers.)
	A.	The intended system name
	B.	The wireless SSID for the radio network
	C.	A unique IP address for the AP (if not connected to a DHCP server)
	E.	A default gateway address and subnet mask (if the AP is not on the same subnet as the PC)
	G.	The Simple Network Management Protocol (SNMP) community name and the SNMP file attribute (if SNMP is in use)
	H.	The MAC address from the label on the bottom of the AP, if the IP Setup Utility (IPSU) is in use

4.	List some of the items that you can configure on an AP Ethernet port. (Choose all that are appropriate.)
	A.	Key configuration and statistical information for the Ethernet port on the AP (Ethernet Port)
	B.	Basic identity information for the Ethernet port (Ethernet identification)
	C.	Ethernet port connection speed (Ethernet hardware)
	E.	Settings for protocol filters (Ethernet filters)
	F.	Operational status information for the Ethernet port (Ethernet advanced)
	G.	Form fields to make temporary changes in port status for troubleshooting purposes (Ethernet advanced)

5.	What are three classes of filters that can be set using the Ethernet Protocol Filters page?
	A.	EtherType (IP, ARP, and RARP)
	B.	IP Protocol (TCP, UDP, RIP, and OSPF)
	D.	TCP or UDP port (HTTP = 80 and SMTP = 25)

6.	Which of the following is generally not a function of the AP Web Server Setup page?
	D.	Filter out undesired websites over wireless access

7.	Match the following AP radio pages to their proper functions.
	1. D
	2. E
	3. C
	4. B
	5. A

8. Which of the following connection options are available on Cisco access points?
   D.   All of the above

9. Which of the following can be entered at the system prompt to display a list of commands available for each command mode?
   B.   ?

10. Match the following error messages to their meaning.
   1. B
   2. C
   3. A

11. Which of the following can be entered at the system prompt to recall commands from the history buffer?
   D.   All of the above

12. How often does the ACM read the client adapter status and update the status icon?
   B.   Two seconds

13. Match the access point modes to their descriptions.
   1. B
   2. C
   3. A
   4. D

Chapter 6

1. Which of the following precautions will help ensure good link performance? (Select the best four answers.)
   A.   Minimize the distance between the bridge and the antenna to reduce signal loss.
   B.   Install the bridge away from microwave ovens or other devices that operate in the 2.4-GHz frequency range.
   C.   Review all cautions and warnings in the installation materials.
   E.   Situate the antennas for direct line-of-sight operation.

2. What issues should you balance when planning a wireless bridge implementation? (Choose all that apply.)
   A.   Cost
   B.   Reliability
   E.   Distance
   F.   Data rate

3.   Which item in a wireless bridge does not require periodic reading and updating?
       D.   MAC address

4.   Which of the following items must be on hand to properly install a wireless bridge configuration? (Choose all that apply.)
       A.   The service set identifier (SSID) that will be used to identify the WLAN
       C.   An IP address for the bridge if the network does not use DHCP to assign IP addresses
       D.   A default gateway and an IP subnet mask for the bridge if the network uses subnets
       E.   The MAC address for the bridge, which is printed on the label on the bottom of the bridge and which uniquely identifies the bridge on the WLAN

5.   Identify methods of configuring a bridge. (Choose the best three.)
       A.   The Web browser interface
       C.   The command-line interface (CLI), using a terminal emulator or a Telnet session
       E.   A Simple Network Management Protocol (SNMP) application

6.   Match the following bridge roles to their proper descriptions.
       1. F
       2. A
       3. E
       4. C
       5. D
       6. B

7.   What do the LEDs on the Cisco Aironet 1400 Series Wireless Bridge indicate?
       C.   Install, Radio, Status, and Ethernet

8.   Which of the following features in Cisco IOS Release 12.2(11)JA are supported by the 1400 series bridge?
       F.   None of the above

Chapter 7

1.   What are the two types of antennas referenced for wireless LAN applications?
       B.   Omnidirectional and directional

2.   What type of wireless RF antenna and cable connector does Cisco Aironet use?
       A.   RP-TNC connector

3.   How is antenna gain referenced to a dipole antenna represented?
     C.   dBd

4.   What are the two types of antenna polarization?
     B.   Horizontal and vertical

5.   What solves the problem of multipath fading for WLAN antenna RF signals?
     D.   The antenna diversity setting

Chapter 8

1.   True or False: The SSID is transmitted in clear text form and is not a security feature.
     True.

2.   Which of the following methods is considered a passive attack?
     C.   Reconnaissance attack

3.   Which is the more secure authentication method for an AP?
     B.   Open authentication

4.   Which of the following terms refers to leaving the SSID parameter blank on a wireless client and will associate to any AP regardless of SSID setting on AP?
     A.   "Null" string

5.   What encryption algorithm does WEP use?
     A.   The RC4 algorithm

6.   What is the length of the Initialization Vector (IV) used in WEP?
     A.   24 bits

7.   What is the process of verifying the credentials of a client who wants to join a WLAN?
     B.   Authentication

8.   Which Use of Data Encryption by Stations parameter requires client devices to use WEP when communicating with the AP?
     B.   Full Encryption

9.   Which IEEE standard addresses 802.11 security issues?
     B.   802.1x

10. Which database can the RADIUS server check for user authentication?
     A.   Windows server

11. What port parameter setting is used for the Cisco RADIUS server on the AP?
    B. Port 1645

Chapter 9

1. True or False: A site survey is completed only after the installation of the WLAN.
   False

2. Which industry site is considered the most difficult to survey?
   C. Hospitals

3. Which of the four design requirements is concerned with system redundancy?
   A. Availability

4. What is the proper antenna configuration to use in a point-to-multipoint configuration, where the links are greater than a mile?
   B. Use a high-gain omnidirectional antenna at the main site and use high-gain directional antennas at the remotes sites.

5. What can you use instead of carrying one of every length of cable, lightning arrestors, splitters, and other accessories?
   A. Outfit the site survey kit with an antenna attenuator.

Chapter 10

1. What device can you use to check the site survey area for interference?
   B. RF spectrum analyzer

2. For a standard survey, how much overlap is usually sufficient to provide for smooth, transparent handoffs?
   B. 15%

3. How many nonoverlapping channels are used in 802.11b WLANs?
   B. 3

4. True or False: Water is good for antenna connections and amplifies the RF signal better.
   False

5. Which of the following WLAN devices add gain to the WLAN antenna system?
   A. Antenna

Chapter 11

1. What process takes the greatest percentage of a network engineer's time?
   B. Troubleshooting the network

2. Which of the following are considered Layer 2 problems? (Choose all that apply.)
   A. Improperly configured Ethernet interfaces
   C. Improperly configured serial interfaces
   E. Improper clock rate settings on serial interfaces

3. Which of the following commands is most appropriately used to find the IP address of a host?
   C. **ipconfig**

4. Which of the following are used to troubleshoot a network problem? (Choose all that apply.)
   A. Volt-ohmmeters
   B. Digital multimeters
   C. OTDR
   D. Cable testers

5. True or False: In many instances, line of sight is not seen to be a problem, particularly for WLAN devices that communicate over short distances.
   True

6. An SNMP-managed network consists of three key components: What are they? (Choose all that apply.)
   A. Managed devices
   B. Agents
   C. Network management systems (NMSs)

7. Which of the following are valid functions that the show command can be used to perform?
   E. All of the above

8. The _____ tool on a Windows NT, 2000, or XP host reports each node a TCP/IP packet crosses on its way to a destination. It essentially does the same thing as the trace command in the Cisco IOS Software.
   C. **tracert**

9. Which item(s) can cause interference and signal degradation?
   D. All of the above

Chapter 12

1. What agency sets the rules for radiated emissions of intentional radiators in the United States?

    C. FCC

2. What is QoS in networking?

    A. QoS means to provide data with the type of transport service that it needs.

3. What association was formed in 1999 to certify interoperability of WLAN products?

    B. WiFi

4. What association or agency promotes the use of wireless networking technology and works to raise consumer awareness regarding the use and availability of WLANs?

    A. WLANA

5. Which agency or organization is a not-for-profit organization whose mission is to produce the telecommunications standards to be used throughout Europe and beyond?

    D. ETSI

6. What agency or organization is an independent, not-for-profit product safety testing and certification organization?

    A. UL

7. Per U.S. FCC regulations, what can UWB devices be used for?

    D. All of the above

8. What are three benefits of Voice over IP? (Select three.)

    A. Cost savings
    B. Open standards
    C. Integrated voice and data networks

Notes

Notes

Notes

Notes

Notes

Notes

Notes

Notes